HELP!
I'M AN IRISH
INNKEEPER

HELP!
I'M AN IRISH INNKEEPER

MAUREEN ERDE

To Rita
Best wishes & hurry
back to Barrow House
Sláinte
Maureen

POOLBEG

Published 1997
by Poolbeg Press Ltd
123 Baldoyle Industrial Estate
Dublin 13, Ireland

© Maureen Erde 1997

The moral right of the author has been asserted.

A catalogue record for this book is available from the British Library.

ISBN 1 85371 756 8

Cover illustration by Tom Roche
Cover design by Poolbeg Group Services Ltd
Set by Poolbeg Group Services Ltd in Galliard 11.5/14.5
Printed by The Guernsey Press Ltd,
Vale, Guernsey, Channel Islands.

A NOTE ON THE AUTHOR

Maureen Erde was born in 1941 in England, and moved to the United States. There she became the youngest Director of Nursing, at the time, of a Regional Medical Centre and later Hospital Administrator. In 1989 she retired from the hospital world and moved to County Kerry, where she now has a guest house.

Acknowledgements

I would like to thank Peter Kelly for introducing me to the Tralee Scribblers' Group. The members of this group gave me the most wonderful encouragement and support. Thank you to everyone especially Frank, Noel and Karen.

Also a special thank you to Aine Lynch who found me my wonderful typist, Brid Dunne. Brid had to almost qualify for sainthood as she worked her way through my volumes of scrawled handwritten papers and transposed my words onto beautiful typewriter pages. Always smiling, always enthusiastic – thank you Brid.

Thank you also to everyone at Poolbeg with special gratitude to Sarah for the beautiful cover, Nicole for her patience and wonderful typesetting and Paula for her interest and enthusiasm.

I have already thanked Allan and Kate by dedicating this book to them but as my poem will probably never compete with anything by Yeats another thank you would certainly not be overdoing it.

With Love

Long ago I saw the magic
And it was so real to me
Then I did not have to worry
About those who could not see

Then it was so very normal
To raise our face up to the sky
Reach our arms out to the mountains
To hear the wind and fairies sigh

And it was so very normal
To believe that our God above
Would give to us mere mortals
Little people with His love

And when I grew and gave them up
And was so old and very wise
No saucers filled with milk to sup
Or fairies hidden in disguise

Then so much joy I gave away
And from my childhood did depart
Then aging slowly till the day
They stole back gently to my heart

*To my husband Allan for giving me back Ireland
and to Kate Cruise O'Brien for giving me the
opportunity to share my story.*

CHAPTER ONE

MEMORIES

When I was four years old my parents told me that they were sending my brother and me to live with our grandmother in Ireland so we would be safe from the Germans. They told me I had been there before but I really didn't remember it very much. They also told me I would live by the sea and play outside whenever I wanted to and never have to sleep in an air-raid shelter again. I wasn't terribly sure about the whole thing but it was exciting getting ready and packing for the trip. And they promised me that if I didn't like it there I could come home at once.

The journey was a wonderful adventure. We crossed the Irish sea in a cattle boat which had big yellow and green stripes around it and my mother told me the stripes were to stop the Germans shooting us. I looked around at the open sea and didn't see a German anywhere. But it was still comforting to know that we had the stripes which I assumed were like some kind of magic protection. I asked my mother why we didn't just put the magic stripes around our home in England, and she just laughed.

When we got off the boat we had a very long train ride but my brother and I entertained ourselves for hours counting horses and cows in the fields that we passed. When we got tired we tried to sleep on the wooden seat planks but each time the train stopped, which was frequently, we were thrown onto the floor.

Finally we arrived in the station in Tralee and, while my mother and brother were pulling the suitcases down from the overhead racks, I looked out onto the platform trying to see who in the crowd might be my grandmother. There were lots of people out there, people getting off the train and people waiting to meet them, and everybody was moving around. Then I saw an old woman in a long black dress with a black shawl over her head coming towards our window. She smiled. She had two teeth in her mouth, one up and one down, and I knew instantly she was a witch . . . I had a picture just like her in my new colouring book!

While I stood frozen in terror, my mother opened the compartment door and threw her arms around this woman . . . I couldn't believe it . . . my grandmother whom I was to live with . . . was a witch!

As we rode in the taxi to the little village of Kilfenora, I kept watching my mother and brother to see if they had realised the same thing I had. They didn't seem to be the least concerned . . . heavens, they even seemed pleased to see her! I had to talk to my mother about this turn of events but I couldn't say a word until I was sure that I wouldn't be overheard.

I was most concerned to see my mother unpacking all my clothes, as it really wasn't necessary. I had already decided to take my chances with the Germans and I was going back home to England. My grandmother's house had only two rooms so it was impossible that evening to speak to my mother alone, but I huddled close to her to be sure that I would be safe.

I must have been very tired from the journey because I woke up the next morning late and, when I looked around, my mother and brother were gone. I realised with horror that I had been left alone with the witch who was leaning over me to get me out of bed. I closed my eyes tight and started screaming, crying and kicking and would not let her near me. She must have gone to get help because when I paused to catch my breath I heard hushed voices in the room having a conference. I peeked with one eye to see what was going on, and my God there were three of them all in black dresses and shawls – there wasn't just one witch for me to deal with . . . I was in the hands of a whole coven! I jumped up in the middle of the bed and yelled at the top of my lungs. I bit, clawed, kicked and scratched any hand, arm or body that came near me. I was fighting for my life and they had the wounds to prove it!

They finally retreated into the kitchen and I promptly took up a more defensive position under the bed where I was prepared to stay for the rest of my life. Fortunately this was not necessary as my mother and brother returned early that evening and a truce was arranged which included biscuits with butter on them and a new dress for my doll which my grandmother had spent the afternoon crocheting.

On those terms I agreed to come out from my place of refuge but I did let it be known that I didn't trust a one of them. One false move and I would be right back under the bed!

Over the next few days I started to lose my fear of my grandmother and her neighbours – oh I was still convinced they were all witches, I wasn't that naive, but they were all so nice and kind and always had buttered biscuits or a sweet handy. After a while I was prepared to be open-minded and consider the possibility that there could be good witches.

But it wasn't long before I woke up one morning and my mother was gone – gone back to England without us and my brother and I were left like Hansel and Gretel in the witch's house to fend for ourselves. I was devastated and would have abandoned myself to an untimely death from starvation under the bed if it hadn't been that my big brother, two years older, was with me and the buttered biscuits and sweets kept coming!

We made some friends in the village roughly our own age and they comforted us in our distress and promised to take care of us. John was my brother's age and the unquestioned leader of the group which, including us, numbered six or seven. John was marvellous and he knew absolutely everything. He was a take charge person and confirmed my question about my grandmother being a witch – he said she was but she would never harm anyone except a person with an evil eye. My brother and I both looked in the mirror without the slightest idea of what it was we were looking for but decided anyway that we didn't have it so we were safe for the time being.

One of our meeting places was in an old goat shed down on the strand across from my grandmother's house and there John told us all about the goat devil. He came there at night and put his claws completely through the building. None of us should even think of being there at dark or we would be done for.

Then he told us about a much more dangerous threat. Even daylight would not protect us from this one. Several times a day a tall skinny man dressed in black wearing a cap and riding a bicycle could be seen coming along the road at the top of the cliff. This sinister prowler was called a guard and when any of us spotted him we were honour-bound to yell a warning and run like hell to hide in the goat shed. This creature prowled the countryside on his bicycle looking for children and if he caught any one of us we would be carried off and never ever seen again . . . or worse. John never said what "or worse" was and we didn't ask. We were far too scared to do so.

John led us across the road into a field of water reeds where we hid from prying adult eyes while he told us stories about the Black and Tans and how they were behind every rock and bush up the hillside. We were not to ever venture into the field without him, for if the Tans didn't get us the bull surely would! Last but not least he told us about the High King of the Devils who lived under the railway bridge at night. This devil could change forms and, if you disturbed him, he turned into a big black dog which would rip you to shreds and eat you but again this only happened at night.

I followed John everywhere. He was obviously my key to survival and I worshipped him – he was so courageous and brave in the face of danger and heavens above, he was so worldly he knew the answer to everything. When my grandmother's goat had two kids, my brother and I adopted one each but one evening I was shocked to see her move the goats over to the old goat shed where "you know who" came with his claws at night. I immediately ran up to John's house. I told his mother that I had urgent business to discuss with John and, although he was eating his supper at the time, he graciously came out to see me and listened to my problem. He thought for a second and then told me, there was nothing to worry about – "goat devils only kill people, they don't kill goats"! Oh, if only I was as old and smart as he was I could maybe have thought of that myself!

But John could not save me from everything. One day my grandmother went to town and told me to mind the turf fire in the stove. I played too long and when I checked the fire it was almost out. I reached up into the cupboard for the clear liquid I had seen my grandmother use and when I found a bottle I poured it on . . . and the fire went out completely. When my grandmother got home she was furious but it was worse when she found that I had used up a bottle of holy water, blessed in Rome by the Pope which she had been saving for her deathbed! I ran and hid in the goat shed but had to surrender at twilight. After having weighed my chances of survival between the goat devil and my grandmother I reluctantly chose the latter . . . but for days after I received my punishment I was convinced I had made the wrong decision!

And John couldn't help me the evening my grandmother sent me up to my uncle's farm with a message. When I was leaving the geese came after me so I ran into the barn and I waited and waited for them to go away but it was almost dark when I finally ventured out. To get home I had to walk down the boreen that went under the railway bridge where the other "you know who" was waiting.

I tiptoed down the hill so "he" wouldn't hear me coming. I was deliberately saving my energy until I got just to the bridge, then I was going to take off and run as fast as I possibly could until I was home. I did exactly that but, as I got to the corner to turn into the village and was just starting to slow down, this huge black dog came loping alongside me and I took off again. No matter how fast or furious I ran, this hound of hell just loped along at an easy pace beside me.

With my chest about to burst and my side about to split, I got to my grandmother's cottage and threw myself against the door. It didn't budge. So help me God this lady nailed two planks of wood across the door each night. And then in case an intruder might make it through without her knowing, she placed two rows of empty bottles on the inside which would crash over if the door opened!

When I fell against the door and it didn't budge, I could see those planks of wood in my mind and knew it was all over for me. I collapsed on the doorstep sobbing while the hound of hell licked my face as an appetiser. I don't have much recollection of anything else of that night. I must have fainted, but the next morning there was a beautiful red setter waiting outside the door. He acted as though he was pleased to see me but I knew I had never seen him before – the dog from the previous night had been coal black and as big as a donkey – however there was something a little familiar about the lick I got when I petted that setter's head!

As time went by I started to spend my days in the reality instead of the awe of the goat devil, the King of the Devils, the guard and the Black and Tans. But I was still very surprised at my grandmother's response to a frightening nightmare I had one night. I dreamt that the curtains came down and walked around the room. But I wasn't sure that it was a dream. Even though John had warned us never to tell adults about these things, I told my grandmother about the curtains and she insisted that I put a stone under my pillow because it was the spirit of an "awake sailor" who had drowned in the bay. The next time the curtains moved I was to throw the stone and call out, "Get thee away and leave me in peace." She assured me this would work and I have no idea whether it would have done or not because once the stone was under my pillow I slept all night. But I really didn't like the idea of a dead sailor in my bedroom and always looked around the room carefully before I went in.

That my grandmother was strange was never a doubt in my mind – after all she was a witch. She put a beautiful china saucer filled with milk outside the door each night and we didn't have a cat – after that she sprinkled the inside of the house with holy water to keep the evil spirits away. But after I got to know that village and the goings-on there, I didn't think it was strange at all that she sprinkled the place. My God, it was a necessity!

Whatever memories I had of my previous life in England faded into oblivion until the first day we went to school. My brother and I had come as strangers to this little village. We came wearing English clothes and with English accents but it wasn't long before our clothes were just as ragged as our friends' and our spirits just as wild. Our little village was very poor – there was plenty of food, but pennies were thin on the ground. The first day of school in Ireland is very easy for me to remember because it was the day I met a Black and Tan face to face and found out what snobbery was all about.

On that day we walked as a straggly group from Kilfenora to the two-roomed schoolhouse in Spa. There was no sense of urgency about getting there. We'd given ourselves plenty of time and we slowed to take in all the new sights along the way. We had never been so far out of the village before and everything was strange and wondrous.

As we got close to Spa, my brother and I stopped to look at a round sign with a cross in the background. We had both been able to read for some time and as we were sounding out the words "Capt John Sullivan RIP Murdered on this spot by the Black and Tans", a brown horse with a black mane put his head over the wall. My God, not only had this creature murdered Capt Sullivan, he was waiting around for us! John had told us story after story but he had never told us what a Black and Tan actually looked like. Now I knew and I was off like a shot with my brother fast behind me.

We got to the school yard out of breath and I told the teacher standing there that we should all run for our lives as I had just seen a Black and Tan down the road. She did not react the way I expected at all. I thought she'd be grateful for my warning and rush everyone inside the building for safety. But instead she poured scorn on me and told me I was a silly child without a brain in my head not to know The Tans had left Ireland ages ago. I tried to interrupt to tell her that they must have left one behind because I had just seen him down the road. But she told me to shut up or she'd slap me. Worse still, I noticed all the children present were laughing and sniggering at me. They were all much bigger than I was and the girls had ribbons in their hair and pretty frocks. I instantly felt an outcast.

Once in the classroom we were divided into two groups with the older ones on one side. But the ones on my side were still bigger than me. The teacher who obviously was going to keep me singled out for scorn made me sit at a small table at the front of the room to the side of her desk. I felt isolated and completely alone.

I sat there with my face burning red and tears in my eyes, willing with all my heart and soul for that Black and Tan to come bursting into the room and trample them all and then they'd be sorry! I willed it and willed it and mentally promised him my lunch if he'd just come . . . but he never showed up. John was right, you just never could trust a Black and Tan!

At recess no one asked me to play, so when lunchtime came I went out in the yard and hid behind a tree with my lunch of soda bread and a glass bottle of goat's milk, which had a piece of rolled up newspaper for a stopper. The girls with the ribbons had white sandwiches, drank from thermoses of tea and played skip rope without me. But my torment had only just begun – each day it got worse. My teacher ignored me and I had to hide from the nasty spiteful girls whenever we weren't in the classroom. Neither my brother nor John could help me. The world outside our village was very different . . . and neither could run the risk of being seen with a little girl in tow.

The weekend came at last and we celebrated our freedom on the Saturday by scavenging the hedgerows for the last blackberries of the season. But nothing was going to turn out right for me and I found out that in life nothing can be so bad it can't get worse. I took off my shoes and forgot where I had left them. Then, barefoot and covered in blackberry stains, I climbed over the stile to the road to go home and a pony and trap came by. In that pony and trap, with their father, were two girls from my school, and yes, they had ribbons in their hair and pretty frocks but worse they also had little white gloves on their hands . . . and to my utter horror and shame they saw me.

I dreaded going to school on the Monday and begged my grandmother not to send me but I wouldn't tell her why as somehow I knew that she would feel very hurt. I just couldn't tell her how bad things had been the previous week without a ribbon or pretty frock because she would have been very sad. I certainly couldn't tell her that the situation was considerably worse because I still didn't have a ribbon and pretty frock and now I'd lost my shoes. If I told her about the shoes she would then have murdered me for sure! I thought of my refuge under the bed but time had passed and I could no longer squeeze under it. I thought of the goat shed but I had tried that before and come within an inch of losing my life!

There was no way out. I was simply doomed! I started out down the lane barefoot and prayed to God to take me. I asked Him to do it as quickly as possible and then, when I was feeling the greatest despair of my short life, God gave me my miracle and I have been an incurable optimist ever since: John had found my shoes and was waiting for me up by the road. He had found them the evening before and had not brought them down to me because he didn't want my grandmother to know they had been missing!

Oh how I loved him, red hair and all, he was so totally, utterly wonderful. I would worship him and be his slave for the rest of my life – without John I would have perished so many times and now he had saved me from the most terrible fate of all! I put on my shoes and walked happily to school with my head high and my shoulders back and my whole insides quivering with gratitude and relief.

Later that morning God gave me a second miracle. But before I recognised it as such it almost finished me off! Shortly after class started, a tall man with a cane on his arm walked into the room and everyone stood up, including the teacher. He came to the front of the room and motioned for everyone to sit down and said "Will Maureen and Owen O'Mahony stand up please."

13

I looked across the room. My brother was as ashen as I was and I knew we were going to be executed! I didn't want to say who I was but my brother had already stood up so I had to as well. Then the tall man said, "I went to school with your father and he was a scholar. I shall expect the same of the two of you." Then he turned and left. It took me a few minutes to realise that nothing was going to happen to me, and by that time the teacher had moved my desk so I was closer to the others. She smiled nicely at me and the hair-ribboned group weren't sneering any more. It felt wonderful. Everyone was actually being nice to me and I didn't have the faintest idea why, but I knew it had something to do with the man who had walked into the room. At lunch-time I was invited to play skip-rope with the most prominent of the hair-ribboned bunch and they didn't even make me hold the rope – they let me skip and when I tripped they let me have another go without making me wait my turn!

John explained it all as we walked home, "Sure that was the headmaster who came into the room. They all think you're special because he's looking out for you."

Even though my outlook towards school changed dramatically I was starting to get very homesick and the final straw came when I came home one day and my baby goat was missing. I asked my grandmother where she was and she told me she had sold her to a man who was working on the pipes down on the strand. I was very sad but I knew that my grandmother needed the money and anyone who wanted my goat enough to pay for her would surely give her a good home. A few days later I saw the man back down on the strand so I asked him how was my goat and he said "DELICIOUS" and laughed! What he said hit me like a thunderbolt – this criminal . . . this barbarian . . . this cannibal . . . had eaten my poor baby goat!

I was through, done, finished with Ireland. I could take it no more and I told my father so a few weeks later when he arrived on a visit. He had come to make sure we were all right. He hadn't meant to take us back with him. But I wasn't going to let him leave without me. I told him about the dresses and ribbons and all my misfortunes. But he seemed to think everything was funny until I told him about the stone under my pillow to keep the dead sailor away. I was most confused. He was more upset about the stone than he was about the dead sailor walking around my bedroom. He didn't seem to understand that the stone was my protection. Instead of thanking my grandmother, he was very angry about the whole thing. Somehow I knew I had betrayed her by telling about that stone. But what had been said could not be taken back; the damage had been done and we left for England a few days later.

* * *

I had got my way, but it was a hollow victory. It wasn't long before I missed my grandmother and my little village and my friends. When you play Cowboys and Indians you know it's not real. But when you hide in the rushes from the Black and Tans, run from the guard and cheat the Goat Devil and High Devil King of a victim . . . well that is really real. And when the holy water is sprinkled and prayers are said you know you are safe and sound all snuggled up in bed and with a stone under your pillow as an extra precaution. What more security could anyone want?

It didn't take me long to fall foul of the teacher in my new English school. She left the classroom for a while and all the children started playing and running around the room and when I spotted her out the window coming back I yelled, "Ah, Jaysus Christ, the teacha's comin." Well, she heard me and she had no understanding of the code of my little village – I had been honour-bound to give that warning but was anyone grateful? Not a bit. The kids I had saved from punishment enjoyed seeing my hands slapped and my being stood in the corner for the rest of the afternoon.

My language had also brought me to the attention of the headmistress who, yes, was Irish, and yes was a friend of my father and between the two of them they agreed that I had acquired quite a colourful vocabulary along with some wild ways during my little sojourn in Ireland. All of which would have to change if I was ever to be accepted in polite society again!

The headmistress took me out of my regular class in the afternoons, and sat me in her office for private tuition. She also gave me extra homework and where she left off in the afternoon, my father took up in the evening. They had decided that I was going to get a scholarship to a fancy boarding school where the nuns would educate me and, horror of horrors, teach me to be a lady!

So I was delivered to the nuns at the age of ten and, because I was a little shy, it probably took them all of one week to realise that God had singled them out for a special penance. Some of them took it well and some not so well. But even without John to intervene, the hand of the Lord reached down again and I survived.

You see, we hadn't been sent to Ireland to be safe from the Germans at all – that was just a cover story my parents told me to hide the fact that they were separating! They had sent us to Ireland to live permanently with our grandmother but we weren't supposed to know that at the time. When my father took us back to our home in England, my mother had gone without a trace and I only ever saw her twice again when I was a child.

I went back to Ireland several times for short visits, but the magic was never quite the same. I had grown up without my little village and my friends in my little village had grown up without me. Oh, I still loved the place with all my heart and longed each night in my bed to be back, but with each passing year I felt more like a visitor instead of one who belonged.

The last time I was here as a child was the summer

I was fourteen. I wondered on the train ride from the ferry if I would recognise my grandmother. It had been quite a while since I had last seen her. But when I got to Tralee there she was on the station platform – black dress, black shawl, two teeth – one up and one down. And I was so happy to see her!

She was very much older but so was I. I wore a straw hat, white gloves and stockings with their seams straight. I hid the straw hat when I got to Kilfenora and off came the shoes and stockings. I was down on the strand in a flash, jumping across my rocks with an old pot in hand, to pick periwinkles. They were the most delicious periwinkles in the world, and my grandmother made strange chuckling noises as she watched me eat them, using, as always, her old hat pin to pull the meat from the shell.

Did the nuns make a lady of me? Not a hope. But, to their credit, I can pass for one if I have to. And my father's concern about my learning superstition from my grandmother – well all of the Cistercian order of Holy Ones dead or alive with help from the Pope could not have intervened because my grandmother really was a witch – but a good one, of the most wonderful God-fearing kind.

How I know she was a witch is between her and me. But I strongly suspect that it's in the blood, and that if I'd never met her, I would still want to believe that fairies live in wild flowers and gather in the bluebell glades and fairy forts, and the forces of good and evil are a daily presence and not just confined to a sermon on Sundays. And when you live a simple life beside the sea with the mountains to greet you in the morning, and water from the stream in the meadow, and your light from the moon and the paraffin lamp, and with heat from a turf fire you just know all these things. And when you wake in Kerry on a beautiful spring day, there is such joy in the heart that there is no need for a priest to tell you there is a God in Heaven. You already know it with all your heart and soul, and anyone would be wasting their time to try to convince you that there was not magic and little people all around in this wonderful place and that God smiles down on it all.

And just in case you don't believe my grandmother was a witch, the last time I saw her she told me I would not see her again, but that I would come back to Ireland . . . that I would have a big white house and a husband I loved very much and people all around me. I laughed but I was very nervous as there was a whole world out there and I wanted to see and do it all. I had plans for my life which certainly did not include a little village in Ireland!

Then one day, thirty-five years later, I woke up and so help me here I am in Ireland with a big white house, a wonderful husband, two black dogs and my little goat. And so help me God I have no idea how it happened as it certainly was not planned . . . but the fact of the matter is I probably had no choice.

Help! I'm an Irish Innkeeper!!

PART I

JOURNEY TO A MEADOW

CHAPTER TWO

THE WANDERER'S RETURN

It all started innocently enough when my husband came home with a brochure for a medical meeting in Ireland. I had lived in the USA since I was eighteen and had not been back to Ireland in twenty-eight years. Many things had happened in the time in between. Most of them good, some of them not so good and some of them too awful to even want to remember. But the hand of the Lord always reached down, I not only survived but had done reasonably well. The nuns had had their revenge because I became a director of nursing with so much worry and responsibility that I surely paid for the sins of my youth. But there I was on that March day with a brochure for a trip to Ireland in my hand and I said, "Let's go."

My husband, Allan, had seen a lot of the world when he was in the navy and in his subsequent travels but he had never been to Ireland. He wanted me to describe where we were going, but I could only tell him about my little village of long ago. I could describe Tralee and Kilfenora but nothing else. I did, however, sit down and draw a map of the village and was amazed to find that I could remember every house, bush and wall even though I'd not thought of the place in years.

And as I drew the map and started to describe everything about my little village to Allan, I found myself in quite a dilemma – he kept asking me questions about my family and questions about my family are very complicated to answer.

Now at that time, Allan and I had only been married for six months. We had met as adults both with a career in common and divorce in the past. We both had three grown children and both had "ex's" who were not exactly pleased with us. And if the truth be known they had never been pleased from the beginning which is why we probably had both eventually headed for the hills via the divorce court!

We both knew the immediately important things about each other and had spent most of the time since we had met getting to know each other and enjoying the present. We vaguely knew something about each other's families. Allan had met my father who was then living in Kansas City and I had met his mother and two of his sisters, who lived in New York. We had both met each other's children who lived all over. But we all lived distances apart and there was always going to be plenty of time in the future to fill in the blanks.

But until I drew that map and started to tell Allan about my little village I had never in my adult life told anyone about the place – not even my own sons! I had simply tucked the memory away a very long time before and gone on with my life.

As the memories flooded back I realised that a trip to Ireland meant Allan would have to meet Auntie Frank and pass her scrutiny along with that of the rest of my Irish relatives.

Now even though I had spent the best part of my life at great distance from most anyone related to me, we had all kept in touch through the grapevine and occasional gatherings for funerals and weddings. I knew through my father what was going on with his relatives and, what he didn't tell me, my Auntie May in Boston did.

We were a long distance telephone family and our telephone bills were there to prove it. Actually, to be honest, we were more like a long running soap opera where you could tune in regardless of passage of time and catch up with the main events relatively easily.

And my Auntie Frank – well she was the undisputed matriarch of my father's family just as her mother had been before her. Although my Auntie Frank and her wonderful husband Joe had lived in Boston for a number of years, they went back to Ireland when they retired. If I were to go to Ireland I would have to introduce them to my new husband, Allan. Now that shouldn't seem so bad. But my father's family were old time Irish Catholics and Allan wasn't just my new husband, hell, he was my second one and I hadn't been a widow which meant I had been a divorcee!

If that wasn't bad enough Allan was Jewish and he wasn't exactly going to be standing in line at the altar on Sunday for Holy Communion – but then again neither was I!

I remembered a cousin, who about twenty-five years previously had thrown the whole family into a tizzy, when he announced that he was going to marry a young lady he had met in Tel Aviv. The telephone lines had not stopped buzzing or the mail flowing until it was all explained that his bethrothed was an English Catholic rose who was an airline hostess on holiday in Tel Aviv. Hell, they all instantly overlooked the fact she was English because they were so relieved that she wasn't Jewish, Protestant or, come to think of it . . . a divorcee!

There was nothing I could do about it except cross my fingers, take my chances and warn Allan not to tell Auntie Frank his joke about Golda Meir and the Pope. Actually I suggested that he censor most of his jokes until we saw which way the land lay and I really did feel a little sorry for him when I had to warn him that Dr Schweitzer or Mother Teresa would have a tough time passing Auntie Frank's scrutiny!

As the date for the trip came nearer I became more and more excited, but I also felt a strange apprehension. There was something I was uneasy about which made absolutely no sense to me. And it wasn't Auntie Frank. We arrived in Shannon on a beautiful morning in May but as we rode to our hotel I had no feeling of elation or pleasure at being back in Ireland. Nothing looked familiar, least of all Dromoland Castle, with its elegance and luxury.

And sure enough when we arrived the Tralee delegation, headed by Auntie Frank, was waiting for us. Not by co-incidence, Auntie May had already arrived from Boston that day as there wasn't a hope she was going to miss Allan being interviewed by the family. We all sat down to lunch in the dining room of the Castle and although I was delighted to see everyone, I was feeling tense. So was Allan.

We had an incredibly snooty continental waiter who gave the impression that he usually only dealt with royalty and was, on this occasion, demeaning himself much against his better judgement. However, we took care of him when he recommended the special of the day, which was poached salmon. My Auntie May, who is a delightful, petite, lady in her seventies, and dresses like a fashion box, looked him right in the eye and said, "Young man, I grew up in this country and as a child I ate enough poached salmon to last me a lifetime."

Our snooty waiter's look of disdain turned first to alarm and then to horror as all of us, with the exception of Allan, fell over the table laughing. In rural Ireland for many, many years long ago, the only salmon most people got to eat was poached and the term poached was not referring to culinary technique! It got even funnier as it was obvious that neither the waiter nor Allan had the faintest idea of what we were laughing about.

The tension was broken and I looked around at my aunts. We were laughing at a shared joke and suddenly there had never been any years in between and I loved them dearly. You see they really weren't aunts. Dora and Frank were sisters and first cousins of my father. May had been married to their brother John and was now a widow. But my father had been orphaned when he was six and had been raised along with his cousins by his aunt. So I knew no other names for them other than Auntie Frank, Aunt Dora, Uncle John and Auntie May. And they all had been young together and grown up together and, for a brief time, my mother had been part of their group.

My Uncle John and Auntie May had moved to London early in their marriage so I had spent a lot of time around them but not so much around Frank and Dora, who were in Ireland and lived in Tralee. My Uncle John had been the greatest storyteller ever in the world and it was pure delight as a child to hear him tell the tales of their childhood. All the wonderful things they got into and all the terrible things they had done to each other and how they had survived the awful poverty of Ireland in the early decades of the century. When I listened to Uncle John everything became real and I felt that I had been there too.

But these were my father's "townie" relatives and had very little to do with my little village of Kilfenora, where my mother's relatives were. I knew all my fathers' relatives very well regardless of time or distance involved but for some strange reason I had only ever known my mother's parents. Once they died I had no source of contact with any other relative on her side of the family

Here I was years later looking at the faces of my lovely aunts whose grace and humor had only got better with time. And as we laughed, Ireland came back into my heart and flooded my brain with memories.

After lunch Allan excused himself from the table to stretch his legs and as he left the dining room, I knew the verdict from Auntie Frank was coming. It was!

"Oh Maureen, he's lovely – what a wonderful charming man and he's so handsome and a doctor too. What in the world did you ever do to deserve him?" Well that's my Auntie Frank, in one fell swoop she had given her seal of approval. Aunt Dora put her hand on my arm and said "Oh Maureen, he's so witty, so charming, such a gentleman and so handsome. Isn't it strange, now, that he's not Irish!" She said that in a tone which implied that she knew with all those qualities he just had to be Irish but a mistake had been made somewhere and he just didn't know it. Yes, Allan had passed his interview with flying colours and I was delighted and when I later told him the verdict he was not only delighted also but downright smug about the whole thing.

When lunch was finally over, my aunts left to go back to Tralee so that Auntie Frank could pronounce her verdict to all the family as well as her neighbours and repeat all the jokes Allan had told her.

Oh yes, including the one about Golda Meir!

In the afternoon of that first day, gloating with the success of our luncheon, Allan and I went out for a walk in the grounds of the castle and I saw the first wild primroses I had seen in twenty-eight years. Much to the surprise of my husband and the bewilderment of some tweed-clad English tourists who were walking behind us, I whooped with delight. They acted as though I had a medical condition but as we walked further and I saw the bluebells, I think they left to call the police!

I spotted the blur of blue through the trees and instantly, I knew what it was. I took off running, screaming and jumping in the air. Now Wordsworth may have had his daffodils but to me as a child there was nothing more magical than finding a bluebell glade. Here I was, a child again, in the fairy glen where the little people live. So much for years of refinement and a university degree, not to mention expensive shoes and a position of authority. I ran amok in the grounds of Dromoland Castle and, for the first time in years didn't give a flip about what anyone thought.

But more surprises were to come. When our tour bus pulled into Killarney I looked around and cried out, "My God! Knoxville, Tennessee". Now the Chamber of Commerce in Killarney might be alarmed at such a response, but hopefully I can explain this to their satisfaction.

I had lived in Jackson, Tennessee for eight years and was director of nursing at the hospital there. Jackson is a beautiful city in the western region of the state. Knoxville is far to the east in the Smokey Mountains. When you live in Jackson, you acknowledge three kinds of people in this world: Yankees, Southerners, and East Tennesseans. The first time I travelled to Knoxville I felt the most intense sadness, which was strange as the countryside was beautiful. As I continued on the highway, deeper into the mountainous region, my sadness turned to horrible gloom and depression. By the time I got to Knoxville I was almost suicidal.

This horrible feeling did not go away until I got back on the interstate and headed home to West Tennessee. As I drove away from the mountains, my gloom lifted slowly. By the time I got to Nashville, I was my normal self. This strange phenomenon happened to me every time I had to go to Knoxville which, unfortunately, occurred more times than I cared to count.

After one trip I absolutely refused to go by myself. Fortunately I had a dear friend and colleague whom I could talk into going with me. Marie Jones and I had been friends from when we first met in Jackson. There are some people whom you meet in life, although very rarely, who you know instantly are "soul mates". Well Marie was one. Although it wasn't until much later that I found out she believed in the little people also, and she's not even Irish.

She would nurse me through the trip and was always considerate enough to pack a bottle of Jack Daniels in the trunk of the car as, to make matters worse, Knoxville was a dry county. She would try to make me laugh and humour me. One memorable night in the Hyatt Regency in Knoxville we damn near polished off a whole bottle of Scotch in our room before dinner. But it was to no avail, and I swear that if I had ever had to stay in Knoxville beyond two days I would have thrown myself in front of a truck rather than bear the misery any longer. And I had absolutely no idea why.

When I saw Killarney that day I knew instantly why Knoxville and the surrounding mountains had caused me misery. When I was a child, Killarney was the main train stop before Tralee. As soon as we got to Killarney, and I saw the mountains towering over the train, I knew that we were almost there. The happiness and excitement for the rest of the train ride was almost unbearable. But Killarney was also the last train stop when I was leaving. When I passed that point I knew my village and grandmother were far behind me. The last time I passed through Killarney, I knew I would never see my grandmother again . . . and I didn't. I know the human brain is capable of incredible things, but I always thought that just applied to everyone else; I never dreamed that my brain could have played such a rotten trick on me without my knowing. But more was to come.

Once I saw Killarney I knew we had to break from

the medical group and head for Kilfenora and that nothing on earth could stand in my way. My husband was wonderful; he didn't grumble a bit about the expensive rooms we had already paid for in Parknasilla. He explained to the group that we would catch up with them in two days and we headed out.

When we got to Tralee I had no idea which way to go, as everything was different. Then I saw a store on a corner with a sign that said "Barretts Victuallers" and I immediately knew my way. My husband was a little dubious but he needn't have worried for, from that spot, I could have found Kilfenora blindfolded.

And suddenly there it was – my little village looking straggly and forlorn and beautiful. I jumped out of the car and ran down to the strand but stopped suddenly in shock and utter confusion – my rocks had gone. Now how in the world could someone have stolen all those huge boulders, including the big flat one which we used for our shop counter game? Then came the biggest shock of all. I looked across the bay and saw my mountains. I instantly knew every crag, sweep, line and where the waterfalls were after the rain, and yet, until that second, they had been completely erased from my conscious mind. Not even when I saw the mountains in Killarney did any memory stir of my beloved Slieve Mish scene. And yet I could draw a map of the village which was perfectly accurate, so how I could possibly have left out the most important part was totally beyond my comprehension. But it had happened and it had happened to me. Yes, the human mind is a strange thing and it is stranger still when it is your own.

We spent two days in the area before rejoining our American group. Everyone asked me questions and wanted me to tell them all about what I had seen. The group thought it was fantastic that I'd gone to visit a place from my childhood as most of them had never been overseas before, let alone to Ireland. Well probably for one of the few times in my life I was lost for words and could not share anything with anyone. I needed time to think and come to terms with my experience as it had had a most profound effect on me. But how do you explain to anyone that the little people have stolen your brain, and not only that, they had waited twenty eight years to bait the trap? And how do you lie down on a psychiatrist's couch and say I have this problem about mountains I had forgotten and my grandmother who was a witch in collusion with the little people and that if someone doesn't lock me up I will have to go back? A little heart-to-heart discussion using that material would have been good for a series of electro-shock therapy! How could I explain to anyone what had happened to me, when I couldn't even explain it to myself?

One thing I knew with certainty was that everything I ever was and had become came out of that little village and that it was now calling me home with a strength that I would not be able to withstand. The strangest part was that I thought I had forgotten all about the place. Yet it had always been there in my heart waiting for me to look up one day and see my glorious mountains once again.

All of this could be put down to mid-life crisis – too much life-stress or a desire to escape from the real world. In the days, weeks and months which followed I closely examined all the possibilities. But whatever the explanation I came up with, I could not overcome the desire to come back to Ireland. My instincts told me that I was embarking on an incredible adventure that I was not quite ready for, but I could not resist. Yes, I was very apprehensive but in a very excited way. I'd opened a door to my past and my future. Despite all of the other options I tried to give myself, I finally did the only sensible thing and I stepped forward into what has turned out to be the most incredible, delightful, scary, profound, exciting, miserable, frustrating, joyous, wondrous experience of my life. And if my poor husband had known in advance what was going to happen, he probably would never have married me. But again he probably had no choice either, and thank heavens as, without him, I would never have had the courage to step through that door.

CHAPTER THREE

MY INHERITANCE

I came back to Ireland just a few months later. I had wanted to come by myself but Allan insisted that I shouldn't travel alone and talked his sister Anne into coming with me. I wasn't quite sure about this as Anne doesn't just live in New York, she lives on Park Avenue and has a summer place in Montauk. She is a true New Yorker . . . the kind who can't believe there is a worthwhile existence outside New York city.

I wanted to come and stay in my own little corner of rural Ireland and I wasn't terribly sure she would like it. I explained to her that I didn't want to stay at Dromoland Castle, The Park Hotel in Kenmare or the Great Southern in Killarney. Actually I wanted to stay at Godleys in Fenit which was certainly not the Ritz Carlton and bringing our own towels was highly recommended! I wanted to go back in time and feel and sense the Ireland I had known. I certainly did not want to stay in a place with a snooty or snobby Maître d'. A clean bed and nice people. Not just nice people but real Irish people was what I was looking for and Godleys was it.

Anne said she really understood and was willing to give it a try, it would be a new experience for her. So we landed at Shannon and I told her that I had never driven a car in Ireland before but that I would try not to kill us both. We had already worked out an agreement that I would not smoke in the car as she had just quit the awful habit and unfortunately I had agreed without realising the stress I was going to feel on Irish roads!

We headed out and, by the time we got to Limerick, my tongue was hanging out for a cigarette but, nevertheless, I kept my promise. However, I broke it thirty minutes down the road but tried to soften the blow by driving with my head hanging out the window!

We finally got to Fenit, and our hotel, where we had nice warm beds waiting for us which was quite a change from Dromoland Castle where Allan and I had had to wait five hours for our room to be ready on the previous trip. Once in my own room I didn't know whether to chain smoke, snuggle in bed or head for Kilfenora. I tried to go to sleep but couldn't so I compromised by chain smoking as I drove to Kilfenora.

It was lovely to drive down the little lane and walk on the strand all by myself and stare with wonder and awe at my mountains – how I could ever have forgotten them was, and still remains, a total mystery to me. The village, with the exception of a few houses, was a ruin and nothing but the past dwelt there. It seemed strange to walk the lane with ghosts and there seemed little chance that I would meet anyone I knew. Well at least the old goatshed was sort of still there and maybe "you know who" still came at night with his claws. But there were no longer any small children around to care if he did or not.

I walked up the lane past ruined houses which looked so small that it seemed impossible anyone could have ever lived in them . . . but they had. And, as I walked, as I looked around, I realised how little I had ever known of the people who had once lived there. I remembered one house where two ladies lived who had a cat and always gave me a sweet or a biscuit when I stopped to talk. And then another house that no one ever lived in, but two men who my grandmother referred to as gurriers or blaggards would come around with a horse and cart and throw things into the cart from the back shed. I have no idea what they were throwing in. My grandmother made us come inside and locked the door but I could always hear the noise.

I walked past John's house which had been deserted for many a year and crossed the road, climbed the stile, crossed the railroad tracks which the train no longer used and climbed the other stile to get to the lane to Katie's farm. Katie was, no doubt, long dead and there was no sign of the cows who had given us our morning milk. The thatched roof of the long, low farmhouse had long since collapsed into the discarded kitchen, where once the smells of baking bread, a turf fire and a large steaming kettle were presided over by lovely, gentle, smiling Kate who always wore a funny hat and britches and never seemed to own a comb.

I went back to my rental car and drove up under the bridge, it was daylight so there was no fear of the "you know who". I passed Peg's house but the door was closed. Peg's door was never closed except at night or when the postmistress came. She used to have a little grocery store in her kitchen and the kettle was always steaming on the range. Some used to say that, when the postmistress cycled into the village and headed for Peg's place first, it wasn't for a cup of tea that the kettle was boiling and we all knew why the door was closed! But it had all been said in humour only and simply as part of village banter.

I drove further up the lane and found the new houses all in a row where once the fort field and the blackberry brambles were. The houses were so close that I had passed the entrance to my uncle's farm before I realized it. I passed the Hickey's farm where the love of my life, for two whole weeks, used to live. The sight of him in the fields working the hay, with his shirt off, would make me blush and my heart go pit-a-pat.

I drove on up to Churchill where the forge had been. I used to ride my uncle's horses there to get them shod. The church was there too and, as I entered it, it was still as cold as ever and the echoes just as loud. A forgotten hankie could never be remedied by a furtive sniff for a runny nose as the walls picked up the sound, magnified it and threw it around the congregation so that one and all, including the priest, turned to glare at the owner which was usually me.

The confessional box was still in its place and the benches outside where we knelt and silently rehearsed our sin list – making up or leaving out whatever we thought would keep the priest happy. He was a terror and his wrath not to be kindled. I always thought it unfair that he always knew who I was because of my English accent!

I wandered over to the graveyard and walked around hoping to find my grandmother's grave but I looked in vain. I was not expecting to find my grandfather's grave as I had heard he had died in the old folks home in Killarney which was the old poor house. I shuddered at the thought that he might be in a pauper's grave. You see there had been terrible bad blood between my father and my mother's parents after my last summer in Ireland.

That summer my mother had shown up out of the blue just as the summer was about to end and it was almost time for me to return to England. When my father heard she had arrived, he suddenly showed up also and may God have helped and given him grace because the poor man was hoping for a reconciliation after nine years of absence. I had only seen my mother once in those years . . . once for a few hours when I was eight years old. She took me out to dinner in London and ordered tomato soup for me as a starter. I tried to tell her that tomato soup would make me sick but she wouldn't listen and made me eat it. And when indeed I threw it up in that fancy restaurant, just like I knew I would, she slapped me in public and I cried which simply made her angrier. I hated her and would have thrown up again just for spite if there had been anything left in my stomach!

When she appeared that last summer she was dressed from head to toe in hand tailored clothes and shoes. Our little village was agog with excitement at the sight of her and declared her to be the most beautiful woman who had ever come out of these parts. But I was not so impressed as I watched her perform for her enthralled audience. Particularly as part of that performance included the role of a doting mother. I certainly had not forgotten the tomato soup! Fortunately that charade didn't last long. In a few days, she asked me to go up to the farm and ride one of the horses down so that she could take my photograph. I did as she had asked but the horse I usually rode wasn't there, so I picked out another one instead and had to chase the damn thing around the field before I could finally corner and saddle it. When at last I was able to control the bucking and snorting enough to coax it down the lane to my grandmother's house, without the brute killing me, I found out that my mother and her friend had just sent me up to the farm so that they could skip off to town without me. Oh well, so much for motherhood and to be honest I preferred the company of the horse!

Over the next few days the situation grew rapidly worse. My father was staying with my Auntie Frank in Tralee. Every day he found some pretext to come out to Kilfenora to see my mother. One day he herded my grandparents and me into a back bedroom to ask our help in convincing my mother to come back to him as his wife!

My grandmother had been kind of deaf ever since I had first known her but in the room that day she had suddenly become stone deaf and kept asking my father to repeat himself. In the confusion my grandfather slipped off to the pub and that only left me – I was in deep trouble and I knew it. My grandparents had no intention of intervening as they had never had any influence over my mother anyway.

I knew that this woman had no intention of ever going back to my father as I had heard too many conversations about my father between her and Clare, her travelling companion. She ridiculed him and thought it funny when he showed up every day like a love-sick puppy.

Now, there I was with a mother who had shown up out of the blue and claimed that she had come to Ireland to see me when, for nine years, she had lived a fourpenny phone call and a two shilling train ride away and had availed of neither. And there I was with a father who had made a mad dash to Ireland to claim back his wife, just as soon as he heard she was here and she hadn't exactly been calling or sending him Christmas cards either!

But worse, oh so very much worse, he expected my grandparents and me to help put everything right for him. Well, I took a cue from my grandparents – my grandmother had suddenly become stone deaf, my grandfather was entrenched in the pub and was probably stone drunk so I joined them in their place of safety the only way I could think of quickly. Hell they weren't going to leave me out there by myself as after all the whole predicament had been caused by *their* daughter.

So I went mute and acted as if the whole situation was just suddenly too much for me to handle, which it was, whereupon my grandmother immediately put me to bed proclaiming that I had a raging summer fever and that she had been worried for days that I had been coming down with it.

She "shooed" my father off back to town and then sat down on the side of my bed and stroked my hair. I turned and we looked at each other briefly. Without saying a word she left to busy herself in the kitchen, but you know something, I'll be damned if she didn't wink with just a faint smile before she turned to go.

That evening my mother wanted to visit some friends. She also wanted to bring me as evidence of her wonderful motherhood, as if I was a scenery prop. She told me to get out of bed and to get dressed and, when Clare started to help me by polishing my shoes, this horrible, horrible woman whom everyone thought was so beautiful and glamorous said, "Clare, let her do it, she's just going to have to learn to do things for herself".

That was when my raging fever became real and I wanted to scream and kill – what the hell did this woman think I had done for most of my life?

There really is no need or reason to go into further details of the dreadful scene other than to say that everything became a total utter disaster just as I had feared. My grandfather stayed drunk and only came home until the pub opened again. My grandmother locked herself in the bedroom for days and wailed – yes I mean really wailed, her heartrending sounds coming through the walls. My father went back to England mad as hell and my mother put on another beautiful outfit for all the world to see, as she made her grand exit, leaving total ruin and devastation in her wake!

She was gone again. My father never forgave my grandparents nor indeed me either. My father was a lovely, gentle man but fate had dealt him a terrible hand. He had lost both his parents within a few months when he was six years old. He had been bounced around between relatives, orphanages, boarding school and whatever. At one stage in his life, when he was a seminary student, studying to be a priest, he thought he had found peace – and then he met my mother. She was the love of his life, his obsession. I know a little part of the sadness that was in him. When I woke up in the night I could see the reflection in the hall from his bedroom light. He rarely slept and, in the dead of the night, when he thought all were asleep, I heard him call my mother's name and I feared for him and wanted to protect him from harm but, young as I was, I knew it was too late – the harm had already been done.

I write this now only to explain the part of my story which comes next. My father did a terribly cruel thing and I can honestly say that it was out of character. If I had to pick three words to describe my father, I would choose gentle, concerned, naive.

So here comes the part of this story which led me to the graveyard that day and probably led me back to Ireland.

My father never forgave my mother's parents. The following year after the terrible fiasco, we received a letter from my grandfather telling us that my grandmother had died. He asked my father if he knew where my mother was. He needed her to sign the insurance papers to be able to pay for the funeral. My father never responded to that letter and forbade me to have any contact with Ireland. I already knew my grandmother had died because, about a week before we received that letter, my father and I had been sitting by the fire one evening and in the lull of conversation I heard my grandmother calling my name as clearly as if she had been standing next to me.

I told my father what had happened and at first he just laughed and said I had been sitting too close to the fire but, when I insisted, and I heard her voice again, he had got very annoyed and cut me off. But I knew he believed me and that was why he was angry. And me, was I surprised or scared when I heard my grandmother's voice? Not at all. She had told me I would know when she was leaving and going on.

My father had thrust that letter from my grandfather at me and said that now it was over. I was not to speak about them ever again. All his hurt and pain was expressed in anger, anger which had made him blind, so blind that he could not see the anguish in my grandfather's scrawled writing. But I had seen it. The letter lay on the dining table for days – a terrible reminder of how weak and helpless I was. I hadn't a penny to my name and no prospects either. I couldn't help my grandfather.

And as I stood in the graveyard that day, oh so many years later, I knew I had to find my grandmother's grave and mark it. And if my grandfather was buried in Killarney, I would have to bring the remains to rest by my grandmother at Churchill for a wrong had been done and I had to make amends.

Now all this may sound sad and rather maudlin but it really wasn't at all. Well, maybe a little bit, but a little sadness is fine, it's the wallowing in it that is unhealthy. And I've lived long enough to know that whatever it may be that brings sadness, even terrible sadness, also has a gentle bittersweetness that if you reach out to touch and open your heart to, it will bring healing and sometimes unexpected joy. Yes, I'm a totally incurable Pollyanna and besides you haven't read the rest of the story!

For the next few days I gave Anne a tour of Kerry. Actually I gave myself one as well. We went places and did things that I had never done before. I even had a glass of Guinness which confirmed my suspicion that it really was liquid shoe polish! But though Anne seemed to be enjoying herself, four days was as much as that New Yorker could take before she suddenly remembered an auction in Sotheby's which she had to get back to and off she went.

I was sorry to see her go. But I could do my own thing and smoke like hell when I wanted to. Besides, I had business to conduct and I wanted to do it by myself. Also Auntie Frank was complaining on the telephone each day that I hadn't given her enough of my time.

The morning that Anne left, I talked to Auntie Frank on the phone and told her about not being able to find my grandmother's grave. She told me to go to the church rectory. They would be able to tell me exactly what I wanted to know. She also told me that as soon as I had taken care of that, she wanted me in town – front row and center. There were a lot of things she wanted to talk to me about – it was an order!

It was very hard to gather up the courage to go back to Churchill because then I knew I would have to really look at the patch of ground where my grandmother, or what was left of her, was buried. I wanted to chicken out and went by Auntie Frank's on the way. She fixed me a cup of coffee and told Uncle Joe to put some brandy in it. Then she sent me on my way with her firm, no nonsense attitude.

I got to the rectory and told the priest's housekeeper what I wanted. She was very kind and took me into a library-like room and pulled down a book from the shelf. It was the record of births, deaths and marriages for the parish for over a hundred years, all contained in one volume. My hands shook as I looked for the date of my grandmother's funeral and while I was looking I found, quite by accident, to my utter joy, that my grandfather was buried there too. The person in charge of the location of graves was the housekeeper's father and she called him to show me the place.

It was cold and windy when I met him in the graveyard and he was so old I was a little worried that he wouldn't make it out of there himself. However, he took me right to the spot and showed me a mound of dirt and overgrown weeds. Ah well, it may not have looked much but by God I swear they had the best location in the place!

The lovely old gentleman, and gentleman he was, started to tell me his memories of my grandparents. I felt the same feeling I had had in the village the previous day when I looked at the ruins of the small houses and realized how little I actually knew about anyone, let alone my grandparents.

When I left the graveyard I felt very confused. I didn't know why I had gone there but I knew that it had to be done. Hell, I hadn't known what I'd wanted by coming back to Ireland in the first place. But when Allan had put that brochure for the medical seminar in my hand, I had been done for. And here I was back again for the second time. I had no idea of what was happening to me.

I was living a totally different life, I was living in a totally different world, what I had looked at and seen in the past few days was not part of that world. But *it was* a part of me which I thought I had tucked away, trampled on and buried. There were so many unconnected thoughts going through my brain that I didn't want to go back to town and Auntie Frank right away. I wanted time to sit down and think. I wanted time to make sense out of the whole damn thing, if such a thing was possible.

I thought I was driving aimlessly but I suddenly found myself in Spa and there was the little shop on the corner, there was the little lane which went down to the bay, and there at the end were my grandfather's rocks. And before I knew it, I had parked the car and I was sitting on those rocks, looking across the bay and the mountains just as I had seen my grandfather do so many times before. Then something absolutely magical happened. I realised with surprise that I had been sitting in that spot for at least twenty minutes and in that time I hadn't thought a thought – not a blooming, bloody thought. My poor brain never had such a rest since first I owned it! I thought it had to be a once-off experience and I had broken the magic by realising what had happened. But no, I was able to slide back into my reverie without any difficulty at all.

I must have spent an hour in that lovely mental state and when I came back to consciousness, I felt incredibly alive and totally refreshed – for the first time in my life I had felt true complete peace. Those Buddhist priests, all those yen and yoga people, work a lifetime for "nirvana". I had reached it just like that and what's more I could skip in and out of it at will, just by looking at the mountains.

When I was ready to think again, I had to laugh. All those years that I had felt sorry for my grandparents because they were old and poor and lived in a little house with no electricity or running water and they never went anywhere except to church or to the neighbours or, for my grandfather, the pub. All those years and I had never realized that they were rich beyond most people's dreams, for they had peace. When I sat and looked at the mountains, I could have it too.

I never would have found that out if I hadn't gone to their grave and been drawn by some instinct to my grandfather's rocks. I wouldn't have needed that peace so badly or found it so certainly, if I hadn't been the age I was.

As I sat there, I realized my grandparents had given me an inheritance which was treasure beyond a price. They had given me back my mountains and my mountains could give me peace.

Being a Pollyanna, or confirmed optimist, didn't mean that I had no troubles. Lord knows by the time I sat down on those rocks, I had more than my share and knew that the chances were there were a hell of a lot more coming. Troubles and woes are part of life and nobody had ever given me the indication that I had the right to expect to get through this world scot free. But it's the perspective that counts and as my husband has expressed it, if I had been the purser on the Titanic I probably would have said to the Captain, "Well look on the bright side, at least the books are balanced." And why not as the damn ship was going to go down anyway!

But even Pollyannas need peace and a rest for the mind, particularly as they get older and the poor ageing brain cells have been badly mistreated. I had been given a gift, exactly what I needed and exactly when I needed it. No wonder I was an optimist. Wonderful things had always happened in my life.

I sat for several hours on those rocks and felt absolutely wonderful. Then I headed into town to Auntie Frank. Now a conversation with Auntie Frank had a definite protocol which never varied. It always started out with a firing of questions. I would try to answer but I would be cut off in mid-sentence. As soon as she had got the information she wanted she would go on to the next question. I swear she had to have made mental lists of exactly what she wanted to know because she kept strictly to the agenda.

We went through the first items on the list.

"How is Jerome [my father]?"

"Oh, doing fine. He seems to have recovered completely from his last heart attack. The doctor says . . . "

"How's his new wife, is she someone he knew a long time?"

"Well I really don't know as . . . "

"Do you see them often?"

"Well, not really as they still live in Kansas city and . . . "

"How's Allan?"

"Oh wonderful, I . . . "

"What did you ever do to deserve him?"

"Auntie Frank, I don't know but I must have done something right. I just . . . "

"You have the luck of the devil. How are your sons?"

"Fine, Mike is . . . "

"How's May – do you still talk to her on the phone every week?"

"Well most every week but . . . "

Auntie Frank could have taught the KGB and the CIA how to interrogate. Give her an hour, and your life story would be picked clean, but the thing about Auntie Frank was that whatever was told to her was never going to be used against you or divulged to others. She wanted to know everything because she really cared, and yes, she really did care.

Nobody in the family was ever offended by her questioning. The most terrible thing that could happen would be if she didn't ask about us. That would mean she wasn't interested or didn't care. And we all wanted Auntie Frank's approval.

Once at a party, one of her nephews was a little drunk and fell over a stack of beer bottles. As he was being pulled out from behind the cases, he asked, "Oh God, did she see me". The person told him not to worry. His mother hadn't been looking that way at all. He said, "I didn't mean my mother – did my Auntie Frank see me?" That story spread rapidly through the family and we all had one hell of a laugh. The person who had the biggest laugh of all was Auntie Frank.

So that afternoon I sat down with Auntie Frank and she picked me clean. I told her all about the graveyard and my grandfather's rocks and of course we got to the topic which could not be avoided – my mother.

Auntie Frank knew most of the story but wanted more of the details. Years afterwards, when we were living in the United States, my father finally decided he wanted to marry again but, being a devout Catholic, he only had two options. One was to seek an annulment and the other was to have my mother declared legally dead. This latter option seemed to be the easiest as no one we knew had heard as much as a peep out of her in twenty years. So my father went to England and employed a legal firm to take care of the proceedings. While he was there, he decided to make a trip to Ireland to visit his cousins, Frank and Dora, in Tralee. One afternoon he and Auntie Frank, Uncle Joe and Aunt Dora went out for a drive to Kilfenora. As they walked around the village, they got into a discussion about which house my mother had come from. Since most of the houses were in ruin, and none of them could be certain, they stopped and asked an elderly man who was walking down the lane which was the house the McCarthys used to live in.

He pointed out the house and, having no idea of who he was speaking to went on to say, "Ah yes, that's where the McCarthys lived – they had a daughter, Joan. She went off to England and married a man from Tralee but he died and she's married to another fellow now – sure she was back a few years ago with her son." So the situation was reversed. My father had just found out it was he that was the one that was dead!

In total shock the four of them went into a little pub in the village to have a drink and ask further questions. They asked the lady who was serving them if she had seen Joan McCarthy when she had been home a few years before. She said she had and went on to tell the same story as the gentleman in the lane about the first husband being dead etc. Now if my father had just kept his mouth shut, he could have got more information but he blew the whole thing by raising his glass and saying, "Well, have you ever seen a dead man drink a pint?"

That was a conversation stopper and the lady disappeared to the back of the bar. My father went back to the US and phoned me in Tennessee on an almost daily basis asking me to come to Ireland and find out more, which I adamantly refused to do. One day he phoned and told me that he had received a letter from his English solicitor which informed him that the records search had shown he had been divorced for some years. My mother had remarried and was managing a pub in London with her current husband. And yes, he wanted me to go to England instead of Ireland! And what did he want me to go to England for – you guessed it – to ask her to consider coming back to him!

I felt like Alice. I had fallen down the rabbit hole and landed right back in the bedroom in Kilfenora on that awful day when my father had cornered my grandparents and myself. It took six months but he finally wore me down. I agreed to go to England. But I insisted that I was only going there to meet her, not as a go-between or envoy. I was going for my own curiosity and also with the hope that in some way the trip would get me permanently out of that damn rabbit hole which I fell down every time my father called!

Well, I went to England and met her and my half brother – it was weird, they were weird. My half brother, who was eighteen at the time, proudly showed me his bedroom which my mother had decorated for him. Pink walls and a four poster bed with a white eyelet lace canopy!

She was strange and rather pathetic with not a trace

of her previous good looks left and her clothes, well they were just very ordinary and really had no taste or style to them. And she was like her clothes – no taste or style – bordering on the crude and vulgar. I stayed with them for just two days and of course my father had to phone while I was there. My presence gave him the excuse. And just when I was hoping to be able to climb out of the rabbit hole, he put a rock over the opening by inviting her to America, not to stay with him, but to come to me in Jackson so that my mother could visit her grandchildren and my father would visit at the same time! I was horrified at the thought but it did occur to me that, if he met her now, this could be the end of it. It also crossed my mind that this could be the end of me and, as it turned out, I wasn't too far wrong.

She and her son arrived in Jackson, Tennessee and within a few days she was on a plane to Kansas City by herself to spend the weekend with my father. When she returned, she and her son had a delightful evening counting the money she had got from my father and deciding how they were going to spend it and also how they were going to go about getting more from him when he arrived the following week. If you think this story is wild, wait until you read on. When my father arrived, I had arranged for him to stay with my ex-husband as I only had two bedrooms. My father was furious with me. He had expected me to put him up in a bedroom with my mother who just happened to be married to another man and was there with her son from that marriage! My father was so angry with me that he didn't speak to me for two years.

And my mother, well I couldn't get rid of her, every time I turned around she was coming back for another trip. In the meantime, I had made a career move and had accepted another position at a hospital in Florida and, yes, she showed up again. Then one December day she called me and asked if my half-brother could come to stay with me. The call came when I was in a particularly euphoric mood. My oldest son had just called from Memphis to tell me he had won a major chess tournament. I said yes to the visit because I was so happy I would have said yes to anything.

I met the young gentleman at the airport and, to my horror, he announced he had "chucked his job" and was coming to stay indefinitely.

And guess what? Surprise, surprise, my mother was leaving her husband and would be joining us in February on a permanent basis also. I was to be their meal ticket – like hell I was! I tolerated the half-brother for about a week while I desperately thought about what I was going to do and then one day I lost my cool and we had a tremendous row.

To cut a long story short, I packed him and his clothes in my car and dumped him at Tampa airport. I was expecting an angry phone call from my mother but it wasn't me she called. She had a few drinks too many on New Year's Eve and called every friend and business associate of mine she had met in Tennessee and Florida and ripped me to shreds verbally. Yes, my life would have been so much simpler if I had been an orphan but I consoled myself with the fact that at least I didn't have her telephone bill! I had no idea exactly how many people she had called and when I told all this to Auntie Frank she smiled and then informed me she had been on the list also!

Since my father went two years without speaking to me, I have no idea what transpired in that time between himself and my mother. It wasn't exactly a topic I wanted to bring up. But when he did start speaking to me again, he had a girlfriend and it wasn't long before they got married. When my mother heard he had remarried, he got his phone call too – she was ferociously angry and threatened to report him to the Catholic church! I guess it really was hard on her. She had lost both her potential American meal tickets at a time when she probably needed them most.

That afternoon when I had brought Auntie Frankie up to date on everything I told her, I wanted to show her my grandfather's rocks. So we took a drive out to Spa and then went on to Kilfenora to eat dinner. The little pub there had been transformed into a beautiful restaurant and the food was, and still is, fabulous. We had a lovely meal with a bottle of wine and as we were getting ready to leave, the owner, Mary O'Sullivan, came over to tell me there was a gentleman in the bar who wanted to meet me.

When I went into the bar this older man came towards me, put his arm around me and said, "I want you to know that I was almost your father! I was madly in love with your mother but she threw me over for your dad". He went on to tell me that he had been so heartsick that he had emigrated to America and later married a lovely lady who was now dead but all these years his heart had longed for his first love. Then he said, "Your mother was the most beautiful woman who ever came out of these parts". I gritted my teeth and held my tongue, wondering if there would be no end to her victims and whether I would ever be free of her.

While I was talking to him, my Auntie Frank became absorbed in a group of farmers who were playing cards for a sheep and I couldn't get her out of the pub. It was late when we left and just before we got into town there was a garda road check up ahead.

I whipped on my seat belt and tried to calculate how long it had been since I had drunk the wine in case I had to pass a breathalyzer test. I figured it would be touch and go! I was greatly relieved when the police officer asked to see my driver's licence and, seeing that it was an American one he said, "Oh you can go on, you're a foreigner". My relief turned instantly to alarm when my Auntie Frank popped up with, "Can I help you, officer? I'm a local". Thankfully he just waved us on – yes my Auntie Frank wanted to know everything, absolutely everything.

I was given a light-hearted scolding by Auntie Frank's daughters for having kept their ageing mother out half the night I was also in for another scolding for monopolizing all her time. I found I just couldn't help myself, I had to take her everywhere with me. We went to the stonemason and ordered the tombstone for my grandparents' grave and did all kinds of things together. She was no longer my aunt. She was my friend, but a tough one! When I told her that I wanted to buy an old cottage, she instantly wanted to know why in the world I would want one in Ireland. I tried to explain that I wouldn't always be working and that at some point we would retire. I wanted a little place in Ireland where we could come and stay occasionally. She brushed this off by saying, "With your fine job what would you want to retire for and what about Allan, he'd never give up being a doctor surely."

I couldn't tell her that our retirement date was planned. It had to be a secret just in case we changed our minds. But I did talk her into coming with me to look at some old cottages.

She almost collapsed with horror when I showed her some of the houses I was going to choose from. She simply couldn't believe that I was even considering buying one of them instead of a nice new fancy bungalow. She was very proud of me and bragged about me constantly to all the neighbours, and anyone else who would listen. If I bought anything but the best it would destroy the image of me she had built up.

I tried to reassure her that I would fix an old house up so beautifully that she wouldn't lose face with the neighbours. But she insisted that I should buy a new bungalow. And I insisted that I wouldn't.

The day before I was to leave Ireland I went back out again to the rocks at Spa and then took one last trip up to Churchill and down the boreen to Kilfenora. As I passed Peg's door I was surprised to see it open. I stopped the car and walked to the doorway. I peered in and there was Peg. The same black dress and the same huge kettle on the range. As I walked in, I asked if she remembered me. She looked at me as if she was trying to figure out who I was and then suddenly she exclaimed, "Oh my God, you're Maureen, Joan's daughter – is it you? It is really you, are you really here? Ah, I thought I'd never see you again in my life, I'd heard nothing of you for years. When did you get here? And then she let the cat out of the bag by saying, "Are you enjoying your stay out at Godleys?"

She had known I was here all the time! Her face was the first one that I had seen that had belonged to my past in that little village and I felt overwhelmed with tenderness towards this frail, very elderly lady. But she blew that with her next sentence!

"Your mother was the most beautiful woman to ever come out of these parts and you look just like your grandfather!" Ah, Peg hadn't changed a bit! She had a very cutting tongue when she chose and had hurt my feelings on many occasions when I was young. But now her words gave me sheer pleasure and delight. I laughed out loud and thanked her for the compliment because my grandfather was a fine handsome man who had fine handsome ways and I was proud to be his grandaughter.

I had finally met someone from those long-ago days who knew me as a small child, when I had been part of the village, and now I was a little part of it again. I had found what I was looking for. I wanted Ireland back in my life and I knew that I would not give up my mountains ever, ever again. And I had to have a little house here. Just a little old house that I could smother with love and attention, which would be my little retreat when the world bashed me around too hard and I needed to come back to my mountains for refreshment for my body and soul. I was going to claim my inheritance and, although I didn't know it at that time, I was too far deep into this adventure. The point of no return had been long since past. The magic of Ireland and the little people had me firmly in a grasp and would never let go of me again.

CHAPTER FOUR

THE PLOT THICKENS

Six months later we were back in Ireland and this time we brought our own medical group. I had put together a package tour which included guest speakers and visits to Irish hospitals which made the whole thing tax deductible. But, better still, I had organised the whole thing so that the tour participants would truly get to see the real Ireland at a reasonable price. And it wasn't all a coincidence that I based the group in Fenit right next to my little village of Kilfenora so that I could enjoy being there for a whole ten days.

I had put the medical group together because, on that first trip for the seminar, I had spent each day making comments to Allan about how poorly organized the whole thing was and how I would have done it if it had been my group to take care of. He finally got tired of listening to me so he said, "Well, why don't you do it then and arrange your own group". So I did and I was absolutely right because it turned out to be a brilliant success and also another excuse to come back to Ireland.

While we were here, unbeknownst to Auntie Frank, I bought an old grungy three room cottage which I had fallen in love with and I spent my nights mentally painting and refurbishing it. I changed my mind every night about the colour of the roses that I would have growing around the front door and I couldn't decide if I would have chickens or a vegetable garden or both.

I also changed my mind every night about just how I was going to tell Auntie Frank what I had done as she had been sending me listing after listing of beautiful new expensive bungalows and was expecting me to make a decision very shortly as to which one I would buy!

Allan was also a little bit of a problem. Now my husband is wonderful but he has no imagination. He wasn't sure if he was amused or horrified by my purchase. I explained to him that I could fix it up and, when we retired in five years time, maybe we could spend some time there. He then told me he would only spend a night in that house if he was hiding from the police! Undaunted, I went on to explain that it was an excellent purchase as the dollar at that time was even to the pound. It was at this point that the trap was sprung and the little people had the opening they were waiting for. My husband became their pawn because we were now talking his language.

He pointed across the bay and said, "Now if you

really want to invest in Irish property you should buy that place." That place was Barrow House, a huge, sad ruin left over from 1723 which had had a "for sale" sign pinned on it for five years. He insisted that we go over to look at it and instant love I did not feel. All I could see was the work the house and grounds needed and all the complications that would be involved. When I asked what in the world I would do with the place he told me that I didn't need to do anything but sit on it as it had seven and a half acres right on the water with the most incredible view. Besides, the fabulous Tralee Golf Club designed by Arnold Palmer had just been established right next door, and last but not least the dollar was even to the pound. I was hoisted with my own petard!

I really did not want to buy the place as I was happy mentally planting roses around my little cottage. Also the place was going up for sale at a public auction. Not only had I never bid at an auction, but I didn't have the faintest idea of what the place was worth, so I took the easy way out and dropped the whole subject. And Lord knows I had had enough trouble explaining to my Auntie Frank that I had bought a grungy little cottage without risking apoplexy for her by mentioning any interest in Barrow House. She had taken the news about the cottage with an air of resigned defeat and when she visited it, she looked with almost disgust at my lovely little one hundred and fifty year old treasure and announced: "Sure you'll never be able to do anything with it." "Auntie Frank," I argued, "You'll be having tea in my kitchen in my beautiful house before you know it."

"Huh," she replied, "I'll be in Rath [the cemetery in Tralee] before you'll ever be able to do a thing with this place."

I just smiled and dug my heels in further and said, "Not a hope Auntie Frank because, as tough and strong as you are, there's not a chance you're going there soon and all I need is a little time and then I'll serve the tea so hot it'll scald you if you don't watch out and, if you ever do anything so terrible as die before I serve you tea in my kitchen, I'll have to go over to Rath and dig you up."

And she had smiled her lovely satisfied smile because she knew beyond a doubt that she would have tea in my Irish kitchen or I'd be in Rath myself with the effort.

But things were not to be so simple and, just when I had Auntie Frank settled down about my grungy little cottage, it turned out that Barrow House was the house that followed me home and the little people were not going to let me off that easily.

I had been back in the USA about three weeks when I received a letter from the estate agent telling me that the property had not reached the reserve price at the auction and was still for sale. He also told me what the biggest offer had been so I had some idea how much it would take to buy the place. I was hooked – I made up my mind to buy Barrow House.

There was just one other little handicap which I haven't mentioned and that was I didn't have the money!

When my husband suggested that I buy the property he meant that I should pay for it, but I had just spent most of my liquid assets on a grungy little three room cottage across the bay that nobody else but me could love and which didn't even have its roses yet. When I pointed out this slight inconvenience, my husband suggested I do what anyone else has to do when they need money – borrow from a bank! Now my husband is a very good businessman with his own money and I had an excellent reputation as a good businesswoman with other people's money. I had always been a paid employee and, although I was responsible for handling a huge payroll and income-expense budget, there is truly a difference when the dice you are rolling are your own! To look at a computer printout of income and expenses involving millions, the only evidence of which are numbers on paper, is a hell of a lot different from looking at your own bank balance! It is so much easier to make financial decisions without fear when it's not real money but numbers from a computer printout which an accounting department can put into unintelligible terms for board meetings and the computer department can display in mountains of irrelevant paper reports.

I could go on and on but, to put it plainly, I went into shock just at the thought of borrowing that kind of money and exposing myself to that much risk. I don't think I would have got over this shock if it wasn't for the fact that I have never been able to resist a challenge. One day this will probably be seen as a fatal flaw in my character but so far I have got away with it, although sometimes only barely and in case I sound too arrogant I am very cognizant of the fact that I still have time to meet my Waterloo.

But the die was cast and I was determined to buy Barrow House. I will be honest and admit here what my first motivation was. If I could have walked away and never seen this section of the world again I would never have considered taking on the challenge. But I had bought my little cottage and I knew that I would have to look across the bay and see someone else possibly doing terrible things with this beautiful old place and, worse still, someone else making lots of money. At that time my motivation was greed – pure raw ugly naked greed. I wanted the place before anyone else could have it and I was going to just let it increase in value and then cash in my chips. But fate or the little people had other plans and at this point I was just being softened up and sucked in.

So I went back to Tralee and sat down in front of Trevor Giles, the owner of the estate agency, and made my offer. I did fine until I had to actually state the number and then I choked a little as I spluttered the words. Trevor was marvellous, he kept an absolutely poker face and asked me if that offer was just for the main house or whether it included the land as well. I might have panicked at that point but my husband intervened and calmly stated that it was for the whole property. Trevor accepted that with the same expressionless face and said that he would relay that to the owners.

Twenty-four hours later they accepted my offer, I had made the down payment and did not have the faintest idea where the bulk of the money was coming from!

When I received the acceptance call at our hotel my husband had gone to Shannon to meet some friends so I left a note: "Gone to walk my fields, signed the mistress of Barrow, see you there." I stopped in town and bought a pair of wellington boots and stopped again at the Tankard restaurant in Kilfenora. It wasn't open until evening, but Mary O'Sullivan, one of the owners, was out front planting some bedding flowers and I told her my news and that I wanted glasses and a bottle of champagne. Armed with my supplies I sped on to Barrow and, as I drove down the driveway, I fell in love with the house I hadn't wanted. I put on my wellies and walked through the fields and I was home – this place was mine. I went down to the old boat quay and sat on the rocks soaking my brain with the mountains and bay and felt the greatest exhilaration and euphoria imaginable. This place was mine, and I didn't care that I didn't know where the balance of the money was coming from for the spell was cast, and if I had had to sell my children into bondage I would have done it because nothing would have stood in my way – fortunately for them it really was unnecessary! But something else had happened that day. I had fallen in love and buying for speculation was out – it was to be mine forever. But I thought it best not to explain this to my husband just yet!

Trevor Giles suggested that I apply for a loan to the Bank of Ireland in Tralee, which I did. Weeks went by but I still had heard nothing. In the meantime I was getting continuous calls from one of the partners who had put Barrow House up for sale. There were six partners, one of whom was in jail for embezzlement. The one who was spokesman and who kept calling me in Florida was a retired priest. I finally phoned to the bank in Tralee and it was then it was suggested that I contact the Bank of Ireland in New York as they were handling the application. I called right away and made an appointment with their senior vice president, Mr Bill Burke, who sounded awfully intimidating on the telephone. As a matter of fact he was downright grouchy and I didn't exactly feel encouraged, but I always like to do business face to face as impressions on the telephone can be erroneous. My little priest called again and I told him I was going to New York on the Monday and that I would know then if the sale could be completed on schedule. I don't think the Rev Father trusted me because when I did get to New York he was there at the bank, waiting for me.

I had all weekend to get ready as I had been advised long ago that one of the secrets of borrowing money is to look as though you don't need it. I had a dress rehearsal and tried on every decent outfit I had until I found the right one. I did my hair, fingernails, toenails and even tidied out my handbag. I reserved first-class round trip tickets which would fly me up in the morning from Florida and back that evening. I splurged to give myself confidence. This was a momentous occasion and I believe if you're going to do it – do it in style.

I got off the plane in New York and sat into a taxi cab and told the driver in a somewhat grand tone to take me to the Bank of Ireland. My taxi driver, recently arrived from Korea, did not speak English and had no idea where I wanted to go. We had a rather interesting conversation in sign language and pidgin English and were getting nowhere until we passed the Bank of Kuwait. I pointed and said "Bank, Bank." He tried to pull in but I was yelling "Ireland, Ireland." This Korean may have studied geography at school, but I don't think there was any heavy emphasis on Ireland's strategic location!

Now do you have any idea how difficult it is to convey "Ireland" to a Korean? I tried to sing Danny Boy but I am tone deaf and I thought he was going to throw me out of the cab. I tried leprechauns and harps and finally I hit the magic word, "Guinness." With that his face lit up and he promptly deposited me outside Allied Irish Bank, which is not the Bank of Ireland and not on Fifth Avenue. Close but not quite there, I paid him off and caught another taxi.

I told the next driver where I wanted to go and

asked him if he knew where it was and he nodded. Thank God I had finally got one who spoke English. I was so grateful I told him what had happened. He didn't laugh! Instead he started into an explosive harangue in a broken Eastern European accent about how life is not easy and how the hell do these Yanks expect people to speak English when they don't speak it themselves and how they treat immigrants like dirt who are just trying to make a living – oops! me and my big mouth! Fortunately we were by then on Fifth Avenue and outside the Bank of Ireland. The fare was two dollars fifty but I gave him a five dollar bill as conscience money and jumped out.

I recovered my composure and walked in the door of the bank and there was my little priest, all decked out in a clean white collar and black suit fresh from the cleaners, pacing up and down waiting for me. We went upstairs to Bill Burke's office. And the priest's whingeing began. I could have put my foot in his mouth but I was wearing stiletto heels and I didn't want to maim him – I just wanted to shut him up. Finally I received the word that Bill Burke would see me. I got up from my chair and walked to his office door trying desperately to cloak myself with dignity and present a cool, calm, ladylike manner that would not betray the terror I was feeling.

Now Bill Burke is one of those incredibly handsome Irishmen. He is tall, almost arrogant with self confidence, quick to the point, cuts through the bullshit and, being an Irishman, has to have a sense a humour although I found no evidence of it! He is the kind of person I love to do business with, because you know where you stand, so instead of being scared I felt instant confidence.

I gave him my accountant's prepared folder which he glanced at briefly and threw to one side as if it was irrelevant. He then asked me how much I wanted and without batting an eyelid gave me a 50% five year loan at prime rate plus two percent interest rate. I could have hugged him but Mr. Burke did not impress me as the kind of person whom you hug impulsively. I did express my astonishment at completing the matter so quickly to which he replied, "If you do business with underlings it takes time." I could have laughed out loud with delight and pleasure – this man was wonderful.

In the meantime my little priest was hovering at the door and Mr Burke asked him what he wanted. As it turned out he wanted to know if there could be any discount on the interest the partnership had paid on their own loan from the Bank of Ireland. The response as I remember was somewhat scalding, although appropriate, but I really wasn't listening as I had just heard that the price I had agreed to was thirty-six thousand pounds less than the partnership owed for it – happy days. I not only had the money – I had got the first big bargain of my life.

As we left the bank I felt a little sorry for my priest as his ears had been flattened round his head so I invited him to lunch. We went into a very nice restaurant which was close by, but the lobby was packed with waiting businessmen. I asked the maître d' about the chances of getting a table and he looked at me strangely. I didn't know at the time that this was the kind of place where reservations are made months in advance. But this was my lucky day. The maître d' paused for a moment, smiled and said, "Madame, you have such a lovely, happy glow to you if you just wait at the bar I will get you a table." Who says New Yorkers are a cold, hardened people? We had Martinis at the bar and then were given the best table in the place with the most wonderful service.

My poor dismal little priest needed cheering up badly and it was obvious that he was not going to have a moment's peace until the whole transaction was completed and the partnership out from under their debt. He kept worrying out loud that something would happen, that the deal would not go through. So I did it, so help me God I did it. I, who used to be Maureen O'Mahony from the convent boarding school, gave a Catholic priest a very nice but emphatic lecture on the power of faith and optimism. He perked up, enough to ask me to buy the old furniture left in the boat-house apartment on the property for five thousand dollars. This furniture was so ratty and moth-eaten that if it was left there I would have had to pay to have it carted off. I then had to explain to him that he had taken his new-found optimism too far!

When I left the restaurant the sun was shining and

as I stood on Fifth Avenue waiting for a cab I looked around me. I felt so damn good. Here I was, a little kid from Iver Heath, standing on the most famous street in the most famous city in the world with a loan instantly approved for more money than I had ever conceived of borrowing, let alone for a place in Ireland. Here I was flush with success and I had to grin all over and chuckle out loud and tell myself, "You've come a long way, darlin'".

My day of glory was not over yet. A taxi pulled up and, when I got in and told the cabbie I needed to go to the airport, he turned to me and asked, "Where are you from?" When I told him Florida he said, "Lady, you must be the happiest person I have ever met. I drive Fifth Avenue everyday and I'm used to all kinds of people, but I spotted you halfway down the block. Lady, has anyone ever told you that you have a glow all around you?" How could I not just chuckle further with delight, especially as he was a voice student and proceeded to sing opera for me all the way to the airport!

I boarded my Delta flight and sat back in my first class seat, kicked off my shoes, said "yes please" to a glass of champagne and just wallowed in pure happiness. This earth, this world was mine . . . and I had Barrow House too!

When we landed in Orlando I couldn't get my shoes back on my feet without true pain. Not wishing to look like a hick from the Boondocks, my vanity had made me wear a new pair of very high heels for my trip to New York. They looked great, but I was not accustomed to anything but comfortable low heels. But after such a wonderful day feeling so good, I just put my head in the air and walked through Orlando Airport and out to the parking lot in my stockinged feet with shoes in my hand. Once in my car I was in such a hurry to get home to tell my husband my wonderful news that I was caught on radar for speeding. The state trooper evidently was not impressed with my "glow" and gave me a speeding ticket. But not even that could bring me down to earth as I'd had one of the most wonderful days of my life.

It was late when I got home and my husband was asleep, but I woke him up and babbled all the details of my wondrous day. I babbled until I heard him snoring and I had no idea of how much he had missed but it didn't matter as I was going to tell it all again the next day anyway!

I snuggled all happy in my bed and was just drifting off into delicious slumber when I sat up in bed with a shock –

In the dead of the night I had got back my sanity. Cold reason had put its icy fingers through my brain and they were clutching around my heart. I realised that those damn little people had set me up because now, for the first time in many a long year I was going to be in debt. Debt that was not just the average car loan but debt with a capital "D," for a piece of property three thousand miles away that I didn't have a clue what I was going to do with!

I sat up in bed until the feeling of terror passed. The only way I was able to stop the cold sweat was to think of the mountains and bay. Suddenly I remembered an incident that had happened when I was a small child in Ireland. I was in town in Tralee and I found a threepenny bit on the pavement outside a shop. I was going to go in and give it to the shopkeeper when my grandmother said, "It's for yerself – sure if God hadn't intended it for you, do you think he'd have let you find it?"

So in the dark of the night I rationalised that of course I was supposed to buy Barrow House and that everything would be just fine and if it wasn't, I would just have to make it so!

The memory of that little incident with the threepenny bit was very comforting. It's just as well I hadn't remembered at the time the rest of the story – my grandmother had let me buy a penny's worth of sweets and had kept the change!

CHAPTER FIVE

A PRESENCE

Well the worst part, at least so it seemed at the time, was over, but now I had to scrounge from every account where I had squirrelled money for the remaining balance for Barrow House. I had to do it quickly as it was early 1986 and the dollar was weakening every day which meant the cost for Barrow House in Irish punts was going to take more dollars. I did a complete sweep and gathered up cashiers' checks from each of the accounts I had plundered and to top it up I threw in my month's pay cheque!

Not wishing to trust the slow mail for fear the dollar could fall even further, I called Federal Express to pick up my envelope. My secretary, who was helping me get everything together and document it, made the wistful comment as she put the cheques together that she had never handled so much money at one time in her life. She felt considerably better later in the morning when I had to borrow a dollar from her to eat lunch. Yes, that day I learned the full meaning of "Cash poor, land rich" and my secretary had her own values and spirits back in place – she was delighted that she had a paycheque instead of property in Ireland and, never having been there couldn't imagine why anyone would want it.

Now all I had to do was make payments of approximately half my salary for five years, save the other half so I could renovate the place and pray for a generous annual raise. I also told my husband that I would prefer all birthday, anniversary, and Christmas presents in cash and for him not to forget St Valentine's Day, the fourth of July, and possibly Armistice Day!

I still hadn't the faintest idea of what eventually I was going to do with the place or how I was going to go about doing it when I did think of what it was I was going to do! Now this may sound awfully strange but my first goal was to buy Barrow House and then I thought I had five years before we retired to figure out whatever would happen next.

I will admit there were a few more nights when I woke up in a cold, clammy sweat, when the enormity of what I had done swept over me. But the panic of the moment did not last long and truly this only happened a few times.

In case I sound like a total, utter Pollyanna, which I am, I will admit to one aspect that gave me a little concern. Actually it scared the hell out of me. In a nutshell I had bought a house with a ghost. Now before I bought Barrow House, not a soul in the area breathed a word about him but as soon as the deal was closed there was a virtual stampede to let me know about my "house guest". Actually I had already suspected there was a "presence" in the house long before the first person brought the news.

When we were in Ireland making the offer the previous fall my husband had to go back to the US a few days before I did. The day before I left I put my wellies on again and drove out to Barrow House to walk the place one more time. I felt like Anne of Green Gables because I found all kinds of little walkways and hidden gates I had not seen before. But, in the middle of my wanderings, it suddenly hit me that here I was alone in a totally isolated area where no one could hear me if I had to scream for help. There was also a storm blowing up at the end of the bay. All of a sudden I felt spooked.

I went back to my car, which was parked in the courtyard, and sat into it to light a cigarette. As I sat there I gradually got the distinct feeling that I was being watched. I turned my head to look at the house. There, on a second floor window, I thought I saw a shadow. As I stared at it a little longer I knew it was a shadow. Someone was standing to the side of the window, looking down at me. I knew the house was empty. I had the keys and the place had been vacant for years. I quickly decided that it was time for me to drive back to my hotel and tried to close the incident out of my mind. The thought of a ghost was far too unsettling to even consider.

My next trip back to Ireland was a number of months later after I became the owner. A friend and I decided we would get away for a week and leave our husbands at their medical practices while we took a break from the world. Actually I planned it and manipulated it so that I could come back. Janie, my friend, who was married to one of my husband's business associates at the time, is one of those delightful people who, if you said "Let's go to Mongolia," would have her bags packed and be waiting by the door in twenty minutes flat.

She and her husband Bill had been friends of ours for a long time but neither one had been to Ireland with us. For Janie it was a totally new experience and she was there when we walked the neighbourhood and sat in the pub and listened to everyone tell me about my ghost. I pooh-poohed the information because One, I didn't want to have my fears reinforced, and Two, I wasn't going to give anyone the satisfaction of the telling because they obviously were enjoying it. Janie however was totally enchanted by the whole thing.

She thought it was wonderful that I had a ghost. She and her husband had invested heavily in real estate property in the USA and she had just seen Barrow House and agreed that it was a wonderful investment. But after she heard about the ghost she couldn't believe my good fortune. She could not wait to meet him!

I wasn't as happy as she was about my good fortune and I really did not want her talking so happily about my ghost.

I have always been very superstitious and very cautious about the supernatural. After all, I had had a dead sailor in my bedroom as a small child, and I didn't want any more of those goings on!! I also at one point in my life had become very curious about spiritualism and parapsychology. I had checked out a number of books from the local library and proceeded to read one late at night in my kitchen. I was on a chapter about spirits being more likely to be able to make contact with people who have open minds, or who believe in them. The thought crossed my mind that I hoped reading about that stuff would not give the wrong impression to the spirit world and have them come calling on me, as I only wanted to read about it . . . I certainly didn't want to participate!

I just reached the part about the techniques used to communicate, like tapping and knocking on walls, when there was a knock on the door behind me and as I fainted out of the chair I saw my young son come toddling through the doorway in his pyjamas looking for a drink of water!

My terror taught me a lesson. Although I believe in a life after death and a dimension to this life other than what we know or understand, I had enough problems dealing with my daily existence. I certainly did not want someone dropping in from another realm to complicate what was already complicated enough. So the books went back to the library and I have never been tempted to read anything the least bit related to that topic since – I am just too vulnerable, as I really do believe in a spirit world but I want them to stay to their side and I'll keep to mine.

Now here I was years later. Janie was positively ecstatic about my bloody ghost, and I had the horrible feeling that her enthusiasm and acknowledgement of him was going to encourage him to become a reality.

The more I tried to discourage her, the funnier she thought it was. I didn't think it funny at all – to me this was serious stuff.

The third night of our stay we were tucked up in our twin-bedded room at the hotel. Janie was sound asleep and I was just lightly dozing when I heard a noise. My body went on instant alert waiting to hear the noise again so that I could locate and identify its source. Dear Lord, I heard the noise again and froze in horror – it was a ghost making a moaning sound. Janie had brought it on our heads so much that the damn thing had followed us to the Ballygarry House Hotel!

I lay in the hotel bed paralysed with terror. The noise persisted. My heart was pounding wildly and I knew I was in danger of dying of fright. I also knew that I had to act quickly because, if I lay there much longer, I would be incapable of action. My bed was close to the bathroom door and I knew that I had to get a light on quickly. I would have had to fumble for the lamp on the nightstand but the light switch on the bathroom wall would be much easier to reach. I jumped out of bed, and in a merciful instant my hand was on the light switch. I turned to face my ghost and saw nothing but an empty room and Janie sleeping soundly. She must have been dreaming because she was making weird moaning sounds in her sleep. If I hadn't been so relieved I think I would have put a pillow over her face and sat on it.

The next day I took her to Bantry and from then on for the rest of our trip I didn't let her near Barrow House.

However there was one ·other person who finally had to be taken on a tour of my new property . . . yes, Auntie Frank. I had taken the coward's way out and chosen the telephone as my means of confession so she had already known for some months what I had done. She hadn't said much when I told her but I had hoped at the time that the choking and spluttering noise on the line had been a faulty transatlantic connection. It wasn't!

I tried to put off the inevitable as long as possible, but my few days left in Ireland were running out and I was going to have to face the music sooner or later. When I went to pick up Auntie Frank and Uncle Joe for their viewing of Barrow House, I crept gingerly in the front door, tiptoed down the hallway and slowly put my head around the sitting-room door. There, sitting by the fire, was Auntie Frank, coat on, bag and gloves in her lap waiting for me. Although she had a grim smile on her face she gave herself away because her eyes were twinkling and I knew I was safe from her wrath. However, when she asked, "What in the name of God have you gone and bought now"? I could hardly be honest and say "God only knows"!

Instead I said, "Come on, Aunt Frank, you'll love it – the place is beautiful". And beautiful it was. When we got to Barrow House the sun was shining, the tide was in and the mountains glorious. It was as though the whole place was performing for Auntie Frank – even the birds were singing and to top it off there were blossoms on the overgrown shrubbery. Now that wasn't bad for a day in November when it had been raining cats and dogs and cold for the previous week.

She had her guided tour and took in every detail, shaking her head and exclaiming at intervals "It's beautiful, Maureen." I felt more and more elated until we finally got into the car to leave and she said, "It's beautiful, Maureen, but what on earth are you going to do with it?"

How could I explain to my Auntie Frank, of all people, that I didn't have the slightest idea of what I was going to do with it. I simply smiled and said, "Wait and see."

Later that evening when we were all out having a lovely farewell dinner, Auntie Frank brought up the topic again. "It's beautiful, Maureen, but what on earth are you going to do with it"? But this time she added, "And you know you have a ghost in the house."

Janie promptly responded, "Yes we heard all about it. Isn't it wonderful?"

Suddenly I wasn't hungry anymore. The scallops in my stomach were fighting with the wine sauce but I laughed and said, "Yes, isn't it wonderful and it didn't cost an extra penny."

Later that night the scallops went down the toilet but thankfully Janie was making strange noises and was too sound asleep to hear the sounds of my stomach wrenching.

CHAPTER SIX

CONFRONTATION

We returned to the US and I tried for months to put the ghost out of my mind. But, just when I was able to laugh about the whole thing, he came back, bigger and stronger than ever!

I was walking down a hallway in the hospital and ran into one of my friends who had just come back from a golfing trip to Ireland with her husband. While they were there, they'd stopped to see Barrow House. Joyce's first words to me were, "Do you know you have a ghost?" She was just as excited as Janie. She went on to tell me about this lovely man they had met down on the beach who knew the history of the house and who had spent two hours telling them all about my ghost. I listened to Joyce's account of his tales and did not like them one bit.

I was in a very aggravating position. I had bought a house which was going to cost me an arm and a leg. If it really did have a ghost, there was not a chance I could spend a night there – the whole situation just didn't seem quite fair.

The more I thought about it, the angrier I got. I tried to tell myself that I didn't believe in ghosts, but superstition is buried deep within me. My rational conscious mind said "stuff and nonsense." But there was a little persistent voice which said, "Oh my God, a ghost – you really have a ghost. You'd be a fool to go near the damn place!"

I battled with myself as I had to find a solution. I considered calling in a priest as an exorcist, but, not knowing anything about this kind of thing, I had no idea how long the banishing would last. For all I knew the ghost could be back in the house in a month, and a little bit peeved about being run off in the first place.

I couldn't sell the house as then I would have to admit to my husband that I was scared of a ghost. Besides, discretion may be the better part of valour but I have never ever backed down from a bully in my life. And that is precisely how I was starting to perceive my ghost – if I had one – as a big bully because he had the power to scare me.

I came to the conclusion that I was going to have to come to terms with either myself, my ghost, or the worst scenario possible – both of us. It was something that no one else could do for me. I had to do it myself which meant that I would have to come to Ireland and stay alone at Barrow House.

After thinking that over I decided that actually

staying in the big house was perhaps a little further than my courage should be pushed so I arranged by telephone for the Boat House apartment to be renovated. I planned to stay there for a week the following March.

As I made my arrangements I became more and more courageous. As a matter of fact I became downright bold. I rehearsed brave speeches I was going to deliver to my uninvited guest – if indeed I had one. To be honest there were times when I thought I would be very disappointed if I had gone to all this trouble for nothing. I was going to take my real or fictitious ghost head on and show him or myself that I wasn't the least bit afraid, that I refused to be intimidated under any circumstances.

March came. On the flight over my courage gathered momentum. As I drove from Shannon to Barrow I built up a head of steam. When I drove into the courtyard I parked the car, walked in strides up the front steps, threw open the front door and yelled into the hallway and up the staircase, "Ok, you bastard – you may have everyone around afraid of you, but I'm not. I'm here for a week and you can do your damnedest"

It was a beautiful sunny day, and I felt absolutely marvellous and in total control as I marched with my luggage over to the boat house apartment. The tide was in and the mountains were glorious shades of purple and green. I was going to have a wonderful week actually staying for the first time in my own little boathouse apartment in Ireland, all alone without any interruptions from the outside world.

I unpacked all my clothes and the odds and ends I had brought with me to make the boathouse homey. Then jet lag caught up with me so I took a hot shower, put on my nightgown and reluctantly went to bed.

When I woke up I thought I was still on the plane. Everything was dark. There was a roaring noise and it took me a few seconds to remember where I was. I quickly fumbled for the light switch. The roaring was the wind from a gale which had blown in and, as my eyes became accustomed to the dark outside the front window, I could see the waves crashing across the bay and unleashing their fury against my sea wall. When the light in the sitting-room began to flicker, I realised with horror that if the electricity went I had no candles.

And then the branches of the trees at the side and back of the boat house started scratching against the windows and roof. It was about that time I suddenly remembered I had neglected to install a telephone – yes I had seen this movie before on the late night show, and the horror was I already knew the rest of the plot. The lights would go out and the murderer would slowly enter, dressed in black, wearing leather gloves – it would be either a murderer or a ghost or a vampire. I cursed myself for not having a gun, garlic or holy water. I can laugh now, but it was far from funny at the time. I was so panicked that I was convinced the ghost was after me for having yelled at him. Although I'm still not too sure that he didn't arrange the whole thing to take me down a peg or two!

Whenever I had seen those awful late night movies I would always yell at the heroine to run – why she always stayed in the house and let herself be cornered in a dark room without locking the door was beyond me. But now I know the answer. There were no bloody locks on the doors – mine neither! Oh there were keys in the doors all right, but the locks were painted over and completely useless. As for running, well, that was out of the question. There was only one exit to the boathouse apartment and even if I had got past any murderous fiend waiting outside, I'd have to run down a long dark pathway of swaying trees and bushes to get to my car. That was totally out of the question. I had seen that movie also and the damn car never starts!

So I braved out the night, holed up in my bedroom with the dresser pushed up against the door, six new steak knives as weapons, a bottle of duty free brandy, a carton of cigarettes from the same source and two packets of peanuts, courtesy of Delta Airlines.

After what seemed an eternity, there was never a dawn so beautiful in Ireland as the one which eventually came the next morning. I was alive and the wind had dropped and all the ghouls of the night had vanished back to their underworld. I finished what was left of the brandy and promptly passed out cold on the bed.

I was awakened a number of hours later by a loud knocking on the door. It was my caretaker, Tom, who had come to check on me. I tried to move the dresser away from the door as quietly as possible, but I suspect he knew because the first thing he said was, "Are you alright – you must have been scared over here last night all by yourself." There was something about the smirk on his face that made me assure him that I had been just fine. As a matter of fact I'd stayed up most of the night reading, which was why I was in bed so late in the morning.

When he had said what he did with that particular grin, I realised that not only he, but the whole neighbourhood, knew that I was over here alone, and if I moved into town to a hotel, as I had planned, everyone would know. The story of my hasty departure would be added to their tales of the Barrow House ghost and worse – they would enjoy every bit of it at my expense!

I was in a real fix. Six more nights to go and too stubborn and proud to give in. But at least I felt I had the daylight hours to get myself together before the darkness came again. I used that second day to buy candles, food, wine and books. I considered buying lots of garlic and pilfering a little holy water from the font at the church but decided that was too crazy to even think about. It's amazing how much courage and sanity daylight can bring. I did not feel the least bit nervous going to and from my car parked in the front courtyard, a bit sheepish maybe. I certainly didn't look up at the big house just in case himself would be up there laughing at me.

The second night wasn't nearly as bad. I'd had time to get the whole situation under control. Being a somewhat logical person, on occasions, I analysed my problem and divided my fears into two categories: human, and . . . well . . . the other.

For the murderer who might be loose prowling the grounds to break in, I simply moved all the furniture from the spare bedroom into the hallway and up against the door. As this was the only exit, I knotted sheets to throw out my bedroom window, in case of fire. I then had a nice leisurely dinner, opened a bottle of wine, and settled down to read.

Now everyone knows that no self-respecting ghost starts wandering until midnight, and is off the streets well before daylight, which meant that I had roughly six hours to worry about any visitor of that kind. At midnight, I opened another bottle of wine, pushed my bed and dresser against my bedroom door just in case the furniture in the hall would not be sufficient – put the six steak knives under my pillow, and proceeded to repeat time after time until I fell asleep " – Yea, though I walk through the shadow of the valley of death, I shall fear no evil; for the Lord is my shepherd and I shall not want."

You know something. I not only slept like a baby, but I had won the first round!

CHAPTER SEVEN

REVELATIONS

The next morning the sky was grey with a heavy overcast of threatening clouds, but there was a lovely warm wind so I decided to take a walk. I circled the fields and the overgrown gardens and surveyed the house from the outside. March in Ireland on a grey day with no leaves on the trees is not the most beautiful sight. My fields and grounds were miserable and unkempt looking. The big house looked totally unloved and wretched.

I reluctantly put my key in the front door, walked in and sat down on the staircase in the front hallway and felt totally overwhelmed. The full impact of what I had taken on in buying this place hit me in one wallop.

Everywhere I looked I saw nothing but money to be spent on an impossible task of restoration and repair on a place three thousand miles from home. I can truly say that this was my lowest point in all my years of owning Barrow House. In my despair I

started talking to my ghost. I told him how I didn't
have the faintest idea of what I was going to do or
how to begin. Before I knew it I was walking through
the house pointing out all the things that needed to
be done. As we went from room to room I poured
out all my concerns and misgivings to my silent
listener. Strange as this may sound, when I finally
paused, I felt in the hushed silence of the empty house
a sadness and an overpowering longing and I realised
that I was probably the last chance this house had to
survive and be loved again.

It had been vacant for almost thirty years and for
sale for seven years before I bought it. Suddenly I
stopped feeling sorry for myself and instead felt a soft
tenderness for this once beautiful house, that had
known joy and laughter and pride and loving care,
only to be reduced to this sad neglected state, stripped
of almost all dignity.

I made another trip through the house, gaining
momentum as I went. All sense of defeat suddenly
went. I didn't have an answer but I had some ideas
and I felt good. I had made friends with my ghost and
I knew that nothing would ever harm me in this place.
It has been my haven of peace ever since.

But my ghost had drawn me in further. I was now
totally committed to the restoration of Barrow House.
I was going to have to provide people, music and
laughter to make the place feel good again. All this
while I lived three thousand miles away, had a full time
job, already owed the Bank of Ireland a very large sum

of money and was married to a man who loved warm climates. How much more complicated could my life get? I needed my ghost like a hole in the head, but I really didn't have a choice. What was happening to me was beyond my control. Each time I had tried to simplify my life since that first trip to Ireland, I was only drawn deeper into utter complication.

Here I was with an incredible project on my hands, debt up to my eyeballs, a husband who loved and trusted me, who thought I was sane, and who looked forward to our future retirement in Hawaii. God help the poor man, for his fate was cast with mine – and what did I do then? I remembered an article I had read a long time ago in *Reader's Digest*. It was about a woman who had bought a house with a back garden that looked like a junk yard. More than anything she wanted to have a beautiful flower garden, and she sat on the back steps of the house telling her little daughter what she would like to have planted, but didn't know where to start and the little girl said "Well, why don't we get a packet of seeds." The title of the article had been "Start at the beginning".

That's just what I did. The driveway looked like hell, so I got my caretaker, and we went to Liscahane Garden Nursery and bought grass seed, flower bulbs and evergreens, and we began at the beginning. The driveway was the entrance to Barrow House and it was the only project I could start on in the few days left to me in Ireland.

Now I really believe that when things are supposed

MAUREEN ERDE

to happen, they happen and that we cause ourselves a
lot of needless anxiety and waste a lot of energy trying
to make things happen when it's simply not in the
cards. After the bulbs and evergreens were planted I
went for an early dinner at the Oyster Tavern in Spa
and met John L (pronounced John Ell).

John L is a delightfully interesting person to talk to
and he told me about a young man who was just
starting out as a builder. I knew I had my man. It was
in the cards!

I spent the next few days feverishly taking photos
and videos of the house and grounds so that I would
have something to work with when I got home.

I made list after list of ideas and the time I had left
in Ireland flew by all too quickly. On the morning I
was to leave I got up very early, so that I would have
plenty of time to pack and take a last walk around.

There was total treachery in the air. The sun was
shining, the trees were in bud, the birds singing, the bay
was smooth and clear as glass with a perfect reflection of
the fields and mountains clearly visible in the water. I
could not bear to leave. How does anyone have the
strength to leave Ireland on a beautiful spring day?

I kept changing my time schedule and telling
myself, "Another ten minutes longer. I can make up
my time on the road." But finally I had no choice. I
reluctantly took my suitcase to the car. I waved up to
the house and gave a thumbs up sign to "you know
who" and headed like a bat out of hell to catch my
flight back to the real world.

My dash to Shannon turned out to be a waste as the flight had been delayed for at least six hours, and by the time we boarded I was tired, cross and cranky. I had my usual early Monday morning meeting at the hospital the next day, and had plenty of time to go over the agenda in my mind while sitting in the departure lounge. I thought about the meeting and some of the people I would have to deal with. I resented the hours I was wasting sitting in an airport, when I could still have been at Barrow. It all made me very aware of the two vastly different worlds I was torn between. I also had no idea how I was going to be able to resolve my situation but I should have known that the answer was waiting right ahead of me.

Mentally and physically exhausted, I settled down in my seat to sleep. But just when I was snoozing nicely, I was rudely disturbed by someone pulling on the back of my seat. After this happened a few times I roused myself enough to figure out what was happening. I found, to my dismay, that a young man from the non-smoking section, who was obviously quite intoxicated, was coming back at intervals to use the seat behind me to smoke a cigarette.

The next time he woke me up I asked him very nicely if he could refrain from pulling on my seat back when he was sitting down, as it was waking me up. That was the wrong move. I was dealing with a drunk, a belligerent, nasty one. He proceeded to smoke more frequently and make even more disturbance when he sat down behind me. He was going out of his way to be obnoxious and included what sounded like IRA marching songs in his performance. It was obvious that I was not going to be able to sleep on the flight and, worse, I had the infuriating experience of watching him come down the aisle towards me with a smirk on his face.

I felt helpless as there seemed to be nothing I could do. There was no point in complaining to the flight attendants as they could hardly throw him off the plane. I got up and went to the galley for something cold to drink. Then I came back to my seat with half a can of Seven-Up in one hand, and a glass with ice and the rest of the Seven-Up in the other. Before sitting down I stood in the aisle and ruefully contemplated the empty seat my tormentor had just vacated, and in a flash from out of the blue, I had the most beautiful – evil – vindictive idea. I looked quickly around the darkened cabin and saw that everyone was either sound asleep or had their eyes glued to the movie. But just to cover myself, I pretended to stumble, and dumped every last drop of the contents of my glass right in the middle of that empty seat! I quickly sat down in my own seat, just in time to look up and see himself staggering down the aisle for another little smoke. I had a sudden sense of remorse brought on by fear that he might have seen me and consequently knock the hell out of me, so I shut my eyes quickly and pretended to be asleep!

He rocked my seat back with elaborate determination, and then must have sat down, because myself and the whole cabin heard the roar. It was exhilarating – this dumb, stupid, obnoxious, drunken bastard roared to the world with complete outrage, "Someone's pissed in my seat!" and repeated the announcement several times as he staggered off back to the non-smoking section.

Now I have had a number of significant happenings which have influenced the course of my life, but this incident ranks way up in the top as it is, without a doubt, the one which turned my life around in my middle age, and resolved any question or danger of mid-life crisis. You see, when that bastard roared, I felt true physical and mental pleasure – every muscle in my body relaxed. My gut unknotted, my coronary arteries dilated, my blood pressure went to normal, my teeth stopped grinding, there was the most stimulating surge of oxygenated blood to my brain. And I knew instantly that the nuns had lied to me! They had brainwashed me and convinced me that I always had to be "bigger" and more noble than the person I was dealing with. I had just found out that constant nobleness is lethal and kills its owner!

Moses had to climb Mount Sinai for his revelation. Hell, I got mine at thirty-one thousand feet on an Aer Lingus flight three hours from Shannon, and two and a half hours from New York, but the heck of it is that once I had realised this my hospital career was over – my use-by date was about to expire and my dilemma, astride two lifestyles, was also over. The decision had been made by me and for me – my ghost, my grandmother, the little people and Ireland had won. It really had been no contest as the decks had been stacked a long, long time ago.

I sat for the rest of the flight chuckling to myself about all the years I had spent being "noble" simply because the nuns had told us that was the way we were supposed to be. I remembered the hockey matches we had played in our school league – all of the schools we played against but one were schools like ours – devoted to producing prim, educated, snobby young ladies. The school which was the exception was a village school whose team was definitely not made up of young ladies – they were killers in gym skirts and armed with hockey sticks! Each year we would have to troop out onto the playing field knowing we were going to be maimed. Because we were young ladies we could never yell foul, but had to pray for the mercy and visual dexterity of the referee. We were tripped, sprawled, and trampled on. But all the time we had to rise above ourselves with dignity and take consolation from the fact that we were conducting ourselves as young ladies and good sports. We were programmed to overcome any thought of whacking our opponents' shins in retaliation. Of course they always beat us with a humiliating score. Our team captain would then have to rally us to shout, "Three cheers for the winner: Hip hip hurray!"

That team captain must be in a psychiatric institution. While we poor souls have probably spent all our lives being impossible pompous asses cloaked in noble righteousness with high blood pressure, ground teeth, knotted guts and migraine headaches. The mongrels on that village team are probably female captains of industry, brilliantly successful stockbrokers, politicians, academics – or else they grace the pages of the society columns in glittering jewels and couture gowns looking years younger than their age and married to titled millionaires.

How different our lives could have been, if the nuns had just one time unleashed us with the cry, "Kill the bitches." If just once we'd been able to strike back at our tormentors without having to feel guilt or loss of honour. But thus we were programmed and each year we trotted out on to the playing field like Christians going into the Roman amphitheatre knowing that God and the nuns were proud of our nobility and sportsmanship, and our intrinsic reward would more than overcome the battered ankles and shins, the occasional broken arm or nose. What awful bullshit. But we swallowed it and the nuns really were proud of us as we had emulated their own aspirations. There was just one problem. They could close their convent gates, but we were going to have to go out and live in the real world. No one had prepared us to deal with thugs in a healthy, competitive manner by beating the shit out of them when the referee wasn't looking!

As I've already said, Moses had to go to the burning bush, and climb Mount Sinai for his divine message. I got mine at thirty-one thousand feet, three hours from Shannon and two and a half hours from New York. I was not going to try to straddle two lifestyles. It was time for a change. I knew beyond a doubt that my little kingdom by the sea was going to be my new career. To bring the house back to life with people and music and laughter was simple. I would turn it into a guesthouse!

My husband had said, emphatically, that he wanted to retire at sixty, and, as he is older than I, I had been concerned that I would not be ready to give up working when his deadline arrived. Now I had the answer. I had all the challenge I needed. A new career and all the benefits of retirement. I would be ready to leave the hospital world. I would have the guest house in the summer. We could do all the travelling to warm climates that Allan wished to do in the winter. But, most of all, I would have the peace and pleasure of my mountains and bay at Barrow. And Allan could have what he wanted also.

Now doesn't all this seem so simple and make so much sense? I came to Ireland to convince myself I didn't have a ghost and, when I met him, he talked me into refurbishing and restoring a huge crumbling ruin. I met a drunk on the flight back and changed my whole career over a can of Seven Up and decided to be an Irish Innkeeper. So now you know exactly how this whole thing came about, but, if you're a little unclear, please don't ask me for clarification, as I'm still a little confused around the edges myself. But that's the way it happened and, as the wheels touched down at Kennedy Airport, I swear I could hear my ghost chuckling away in the hallway of Barrow House!

CHAPTER EIGHT

BLUEBELLS AND MEADOWS

My husband met me at the airport in Orlando and was delighted to see me. I wondered how long that would last when I was to tell him that I had decided to be an Irish Innkeeper when we retired! Actually he took the news very well. In fact he thought it was a brilliant idea so long as I promised that he would never have to spend a winter in Ireland – a promise I readily made, and have only broken a few times under special circumstances!

With his blessing and encouragement, I started to plan just how I could put a guesthouse together. How I could cope with the problem of being four thousand miles away and how to afford it. The agreement was, not just no winters in Ireland, but I had to finance it myself without plundering from capital. The guesthouse would have to be financially independent and not a liability.

Oh well, no guts, no glory – I went for it!

The partnership I had bought Barrow House from

had started the conversion of the house into six apartments and their architect had done a wonderful job of the division and layout. I saw no reason to tamper with the work already done. I was just going to change the word apartments to suites and use them as luxury guesthouse accommodation.

There were six suites, some with one, two and three bedrooms, which meant that groups travelling together could have a large suite with their own bedrooms, bathroom, and sitting-room with fireplace at a fraction of the cost of a luxury hotel and in the most fantastic, scenic location right next to the Tralee Golf Club. Someone once said, "Location is all." I had the location along with a beautiful old house steeped in history. What more could a visitor to Ireland want . . . ?

Well, they were going to want beds, furniture, the roof fixed, the walls patched, the whole place redecorated and the grounds restored just for openers. So I started making more lists. I had looked at Irish furniture when I furnished the boat house apartment and found it to be incredibly expensive and not really what I wanted.

I watched my videos of Barrow House over and over again, and started to make decisions. I picked out a shade of green and had the whole of the inside of my house in Florida painted that shade with a white trim, so I would have something to match colours to. Then I went to one of our hospital board members who owned a very large furniture store, and borrowed some of his manufacturers' catalogues. After weeks of agonising I'd chosen the basic furniture, and the price was such that, even with the cost of shipping, it just didn't cost that much more. And I would have what I wanted.

I had twelve months to get ready before Allan retired, and I absolutely had to have my guest house ready for operation by then. Once I gave up my well-paid position, my purchasing power would be seriously damaged. Not only did I have to have most everything done by May 1989, I also had to have it paid for. I had no guarantee that I would have an abundance of paying customers that first year, and I was going to have to be prepared to float all the expenses of the operation myself.

Allan and I had a strict agreement that the guest house was my retirement project. His project was managing our retirement funds, deciding and handling arrangements for all our winter travel and having all the time to do the things he had planned like canoe down every river in Ireland – oh and of course, he got to decide who would be President of the USA.

When the furniture and colours had been picked out, it was time for me to make another trip to Ireland and get an estimate from an Irish builder. I could only take a week off as I would need to stretch my vacation time throughout the coming year. Allan couldn't go so I asked my dear friend Marie Jones from my Tennessee days if she would like to join me and, in a flash, the response was yes.

I told her she could only bring one suitcase as I needed her baggage allowance for hauling all kinds of assorted items that I was plundering from our Florida home, as well as the results of numerous trips to the Walmart Discount Store. Now Marie is a clothes-horse. She has an outfit for all occasions, but she graciously conceded, and even took it in good grace when I gave her a huge carry-on bag to pretend was hers when we met at the Atlanta airport.

When we got to Shannon and were going through customs, we looked like a Laurel and Hardy act. We were trying to wheel our carts through looking nonchalant, but all the boxes and suitcases kept sliding off onto the floor. We tried to get them back on the cart, but the damn stuff fell back on top of us. At one point we both ended up on the ground. When I looked up, there were three customs officers standing there, with their arms folded, staring at us. They didn't move, or say a word, they just watched this duo of middle-aged ladies scrambling round on the floor, trying to look as if they weren't smuggling.

The boxes and suitcases were packed to the nines with sheets, towels, pillowcases, etc. But we couldn't have acted more guiltily if we were carrying kilos of cocaine. It was almost an insult that they let us through without challenge, as if they took one look at us and decided that these two blondes were incapable of doing anything serious!

After a two hour drive we got to Barrow House. Marie had never been to Ireland before, and she expressed her pleasure every mile of the way – it was pure delight listening to her, or answering her questions, and it was on that trip that we confessed to each other our belief in the little people. When we arrived in the courtyard, the tide was in and the mountains glorious in the sunlight.

We both waved up to the ghost, who was no doubt watching us from the middle window, and started up the side steps to the boathouse. It was then, to Marie's surprise, that I started to scream – there in front of me along the pathway were bluebells everywhere – simply everywhere. We went up to the back of the big house and down through the old orchard and there they were just as thick as the ground could hold them, and just as magically blue as God could make them. Marie realised that I had never seen bluebells there before, and laughed and yelled just as much as I. I had never seen the bluebells before because I had never been to Barrow House in May. It was a wonderful, glorious discovery. Never, never in my life had I owned a bluebell glade – this was my very own glade, not in someone else's woods, not something to have to hunt for, but here on my own grounds – my very own magical bluebell glade. My cup ranneth over and my surrender to Barrow House, my ghost and the little people was total, utter, and complete!

Actually it's just as well I saw the bluebell glade. Shortly thereafter I received the estimate from my builder and if it hadn't been for euphoria induced by the bluebells and topped up by champagne Marie and I were celebrating with, I think I would have been a "goner". Instead I said something to the effect of, "Oh well, in for a penny, in for a pound". I wouldn't swear to it, but I think there was a big sigh of relief from the big house as well as from my builder who had just got his first big job!

I have assigned a whole chapter later in this book to the joys of building in Ireland, but at this point I was as green and innocent as the green grass of Wyoming. It was just as well as if I could have foreseen at one time all the trials, tribulations and robbery which lay ahead I would have sobered up quickly, taken a photo of the bluebells as a souvenir, and headed for Shannon!

But fortunately it didn't happen that way, and myself and Marie just continued with our excitement. We took a lovely long walk along the beach, and met our neighbour Eugie O'Sullivan, who gave us a big bag of potatoes from his field. We boiled a pot that night, and so help me, almost all we ate for the rest of the week were Eugie's potatoes, laden with butter, salt and pepper. As we started to run low we began watching how many the other one was eating. When we were down to the last potato, a fifteen-year friendship was in jeopardy if I hadn't cut it in half!

Here we were, two grown women, used to eating in the finest of restaurants, fighting over a potato, but we did it and did it without shame, as Eugie

O'Sullivan's potatoes are the finest in the world . . .
yes, Ireland does strange things to you!

That last year I made four one-week trips to
Ireland while all the necessary work was going on, and
the frequent flyer miles just piled up almost quicker
than I could use them. The most awful decision I had
to make was the one to replace the roof. The darn
thing was over 200 years old and if it had had the
decency to hold up for another forty years, I would
have been a hell of a lot better off financially. I
wavered and wavered, trying to get all kinds of
different opinions which would tell me what I wanted
to hear. But no one could throw me a lifeline. I finally
told my builder to go up on the roof and smash some
slates and then the die would be cast, and I could turn
my attention to the next issue.

Eventually we got to the actual decoration. I
wanted the outside of the house painted white with
black trim and a yellow door. Everyone including
Allan was aghast when I announced the color I
wanted for the front door. I tried to explain that it
wasn't to be just any old yellow but a beautiful spring
yellow, all to no avail. Absolutely no one agreed with
me and Allan even tried to back up his argument by
telling me that, in China, yellow doors indicate houses
of ill repute presided over by madames. He may have
been making that up but it had no impact on me. I
pointed out that it was most unlikely that we would
have a problem with hordes of Chinese running
around North Kerry flocking down our driveway

misunderstanding exactly what kind of guesthouse I was running. However, it did cross my mind that if the guesthouse didn't pay its way, I might have to consider other creative business options.

I stood firm on the yellow door. Even if my builder, painter and Allan couldn't visualize the effect, it was perfectly obvious to me that the front of the house screamed out for a lovely spring yellow front door.

I sent John Joe a swatch of the green from my Florida walls for the inside of the house which was to be set off by a white trim, made arrangements for the brown carpeting I had already picked out and asked for a time frame when all this, including the roof, would be completed.

I was told this would be done by July 30th 1988. I was so excited I couldn't wait to see the results and, when I announced to my Florida friends that I was going to Ireland in August, I had a chorus of volunteers to go with me. That was wonderful news as I needed their baggage allowance to transport further purchases to my Irish guesthouse. Everyone was most congenial about this and as there were eight of us involved, it meant we could leave them all with one suitcase and have eight large heavy duty cardboard boxes to stash my supplies in and not have to pay extra baggage weight.

We did get rather strange looks at the Delta desk in Orlando as most tourists do not go off to Ireland with eight large boxes in lieu of suitcases. But we simply smiled, acted as though we did this all the time and that there was nothing in the least bit unusual about what we were doing. So they checked in our luggage and tried not to look too inquisitive. But I'm sure they talked about us afterwards.

When we got to Shannon we had to load everything on to a porter's large baggage cart and then began our walk into the customs hall. Now I really do feel European customs officials are totally unfair in the manner in which they conduct business. In the USA everyone goes through a counter area, one at a time, while they check your baggage over. I mean you *know* when you get off a plane in the States that you are going to be eyeball to eyeball with a customs official. But not in Europe. Instead they let you claim your bags from the luggage carousel, pick out the doorway you are going to go through, which is marked according to whether or not you are going to declare anything and, when you have already burned your bridges, committed yourself to being innocent, they wait for you. There are no counters to go through – just a large hall to walk through pushing your luggage while the customs officials stand around in silent groups *watching you,* their eyes roving around trying to spot the gulity. This is pure psychological warfare. I never know whether to look them straight in the eye, look straight ahead, look nonchalantly around the hall or a combination of all three.

That particular morning in Shannon, as I helped Allan to push a huge baggage cart, I did the

115

combination of all of the above. When I did the look them right in the eye bit I recognised one of the customs officials from when Marie and I had done our Laurel and Hardy act a few months previously. He was staring right at me and with a resigned expression and movement of his hand he indicated that I had pushed my luck too far and that he was going to have to check me out.

I told Allan we had to pull over but Allan, intent on pushing the cart to the exit, wanted to argue with me about which direction we should be going. When I finally convinced him that customs wanted to have a little chat with us and we had to pull over he very ungraciously turned the whole baggage cart at right angles directly towards the customs officer, which blocked about three lanes of passengers trying to depart the customs hall.

The customs officer looked at me, looked at the huge baggage cart and the crowd pushing around it and, with utter resignation and disgust said, "What's in the boxes?" I told him it was bed linen and household wares because there were eight of us coming to spend two weeks at a house I owned in Ireland. He pointed to the largest box and said "Open it".

He had to be joking – I had taped and roped those boxes to survive all the baggage handlers and cargo holds. Those boxes weren't something that you could open easily. However Allan, my wonderful Eagle scout, got out his swiss army penknife and started to cut down one seam. He got about six inches down when the customs officer stopped him – looked in the opening, checked the peach colored material visible to the eye which was in fact part of my stock of color co-ordinated sheets – looked at the traffic obstruction we were causing and with a look towards me which said, "Please don't ever do this to me again as I am just doing my job," told us to "go on".

When we got outside the airport and were assembling our stuff ready to load into the rental cars, I looked around at what needed to be found space for and saw bottles and bottles of liquor which certainly didn't belong to us. When I asked where they had come from everyone in our group said they *were ours*. I was stunned as it was way over our legal limit and I could not believe that they had got through customs without being challenged. Allan Shaw smiled, shrugged his shoulders and said, "We just carried it along right in view of everyone and when they pulled you over, we kept walking on through and no one said anything so we thought it must have been all right".

Well God bless Allan Shaw and all our group who did his bidding and kept walking, looking innocent because although they thought they were, he damn sure knew they weren't. Two hours down the road when we got to Barrow House we needed every drop of the hard stuff the good Lord ever allowed to be fermented.

When we drove down the driveway the new roof

looked beautiful but the front of the house looked strange. When we got to the courtyard I realized why. Only half of the outside of the house had been painted. But the half had been divided in quarters – a quarter strip at the top, a quarter strip at the bottom and the middle half waiting for the painter to come back. And my spring yellow front door – black as the ace of spades and newly painted!

With terrible foreboding I walked up the front steps into the hallway. The strangled scream which came out of my mouth and throat brought the others running. But they stopped quickly in horror when they saw what I was looking at. The walls were the most grotesque shade of green I had ever seen. As a nurse I had seen better colours coming out of patients' naso-gastric tubes. I quickly slipped into a four thousand pound shock and staggered over to my boathouse apartment, where I fixed myself the largest, strongest drink I had ever mixed in my life.

I ignored Allan and my friends and sat for hours staring blankly, frozen in horror that I had made a four thousand pound mistake at a point where I could least afford it. Everyone was most supportive and Allan kept rubbing my neck and shoulders while different voices tried to tell me everything was going to be all right, the colour wasn't that bad. Each time anyone said that I just let out a moan!

The next day after I had sat crouched in the same spot for twenty-four hours, moving only to go to the bathroom or the kitchen to fix another drink, Allan came back from a trip to the big house and said, "Honey, please come look at it, I think you'll like it." He pulled me up and led me like a small child over to the front steps and up to the front hallway. I looked in astonishment. It was beautiful, it was gorgeous, it was exactly the colour I had picked out. What I had been looking at the day before had only been the first coat, and it had still been wet. My four thousand pounds was safe. I went back to the boathouse apartment, and passed out cold with relief and exhaustion.

During that twenty-four hours when I had totally ignored my friends they had been busy fending for themselves. Not all the carpeting had been laid but they had picked out finished suites and had moved in. They vacuumed and cleaned up the carpet remnants, scoured their bathrooms removing sand and gravel that for some strange reason had been in the bathtubs and had generally made themselves at home. The only furniture they had to worry about were the new beds I had previously arranged to be delivered over the telephone and they had made these up using, of course, the new sheets and blankets which had just crossed the Atlantic.

They really were a very creative group. They had arranged twin beds in the sittingroom each side of the fireplace, gathered timber for the fire and wild flowers for decoration. They then had issued an invitation for Allan and me to come over for happy hour and when we got there the fire was roaring, candles were lit and a scrumptious array of snacks and hors d'oeuvres were displayed alongside the contraband liquor bottles. The table was made up from two large paint buckets with wooden planks from the builders, tastefully covered with a new peach sheet. The ice bucket was a plastic bag surrounded with ivy and the glasses were an assorted selection of odds and ends includings mugs from my kitchen. The whole thing looked fantastic, a valid testimony to the theory that style and taste cannot be bought – it's in the blood.

So we celebrated Barrow House having its first occupants in thirty years and even had a toast to my wonderful taste in colours. Actually we went on to have toasts to anything Irish we could think of. I almost slipped up and proposed a toast to my "you know who" but decided it might be best not to mention him. I wasn't quite sure they were ready for that. By the end of the evening I had totally recovered from the shock of my arrival. I wasn't even upset about my black door as it was going to be yellow eventually, just as the outside of the house was going to be all white – eventually.

I was starting to catch a glimpse of Irish time. Once I understood it, I was sure I could accept it – eventually!

Well that was August 1988 and, when I came back in October, the house was as ready as it could be without the furniture. The carpeting and curtains were all there, walls and ceilings painted to perfection. Even my front door was yellow. I could not believe the transformation. And all alone and by myself I opened the front door and walked in – it was absolutely beautiful and myself and "you know who" walked through the house together. What a difference from the day, not too long past, when I had walked through feeling total despair. And, as I walked from room to room, it was as if the two of us were gloating with self accomplishment. The only difference was, I had spent a fortune and my "silent partner" had been silent and hadn't spent a penny!

Now all I had to do was tie up some loose ends with one career and move on to the next. This should have seemed difficult but really it wasn't. In those October days at Barrow House, I already knew that February of the following year was my retirement date. If I had not had that date fixed clearly in my mind, I could not have left Ireland that October. I honestly believe I would have simply picked up the telephone and said, "No, I'm not coming back" and not apologized to anyone. But for four months it didn't seem worth the trouble it would have caused and besides I would have missed Allan.

So once more I put my luggage in the car, looked up at the house, gave my thumbs up sign to "you know who" and drove to Shannon, promising myself that this would be the last trip I would ever have to make, unless it be by my choice.

Whenever I had come to Ireland over the last five years, I had felt like a child playing hookey from school – I had a wonderful time but beneath it all was the dread of having to pay the piper for the stolen freedom. I didn't want to pay that price anymore. I had worked for twenty-eight years in an intensive, stressful environment and had thrived on the challenge. Now I wanted time to play in the meadow.

Actually I felt more like a renegade hound dog who no longer wanted to run with the pack – there can be some awful mean hummers in that pack and at the end of the day, who the hell wants a dead fox as a reward? So much nicer to lie by a cosy warm fire in peace and not have to listen to the yapping and baying of the hounds. Or to take a stroll and look at the scenery and chase butterflies instead of running like mad to keep up with the pack, or worse still, scrambling like hell to stay ahead of them. Besides, some of those mean hummers can have fleas or rabies, which in close proximity can be contagious!

To be frank I wanted a new owner and that owner was to be me.

I had seen the bluebells and glimpsed the freedom of the meadow and this old hound dog was ready to leap the fence!

CHAPTER NINE

LEAPING THE FENCE

Now most everyone who has a career has written a letter of resignation at some time. I'm quite certain also that most people have written substantially more letters of resignation in their minds than ones ever committed to paper. The mind ones tend to be more on the order of "Dear Mr or Mrs . . . sod off", while the written ones usually contain more benign use of the English language.

I had changed employment over my career days a number of times and I can honestly say I have never written a letter of resignation with anger or bitterness – relief maybe – but I had never worked in an organization, no matter what the circumstances, where I did not feel I had contributed something of value and likewise something of value had been given to me, like a paycheque!

People now ask me in wonderment and awe how I could walk away from a career in my late forties without regret. I suspect the ones who ask that question are thinking of doing the same thing themselves, but don't know how. In my case it was simple. I don't mean to be facetious at all when I tell them all they have to do is write a letter of resignation when they know what else it is they want to do, it's as simple as that. No one but a moron or someone with a brain tumour wakes up one day and, without any previous thought on the subject, just quits.

The stockbroker who went off on a sailboat around the world and decided to market garden in the Caribbean or the South African architect who took his family and sailboat around the world and opened a coffee shop in the Bay of Islands in New Zealand – I've met both of them and I'll bet my bottom dollar neither of these people just woke up one morning and went out and bought a boat. I'll also bet they fantasised about it for some time and made their fantasy into reality by working and planning to achieve that goal. I mean it's hard to take a sailboat around the world if you don't know how to sail. Rational people don't give up well paid jobs and known security to sit in a boat tied up to a pier or to grow ground nuts in Bora Bora if they don't know where Bora Bora is!

My guess is that most people, once they hit their forties and have been in one profession for all their working life, start looking down the road of the years ahead and begin to have dreams or fantasies of other things they would like to do. Most people just dream and never take practical steps, not because they don't have the courage, but because they really don't want to do it and are simply enjoying the dream. But that doesn't stop them being envious of someone who actually does!

I had been very fortunate in my working career. I had thoroughly enjoyed it. However, like most people, I had had my ups and downs and for a period of time before I met Allan I was stuck in a very unpleasant situation which was so bad I even fantasised about becoming a bag lady rather than continue what I was doing. I didn't become a bag lady because, while there would be complete freedom from responsibility and no bills to pay, the fun of sleeping on park benches or rummaging in garbage cans would not have given me the rewards of a clean bed and a nice meal which my current paycheque did.

But having my fantasy was fun and healthy – it was only when the park bench and garbage cans started looking better that I got scared. When that scenario started looking good, I knew I was in deep trouble!

The whole secret of making a complete change of career and lifestyle in middle age is when there are greater personal rewards involved by doing so – and that's it in a nutshell. I had been concerned that I would not be able to give up the hospital world when Allan retired. And then I bought Barrow House. I've told you some of the circumstances which influenced my thinking. It also did something else for me. Because in 1985 I knew I was a "short timer," with only three hospital career years left, I was able to accept a position that no one in their right mind would have taken as it would be the kiss of death to any career – mine included – if I had planned to stay around.

But under the circumstances I was delighted to take the risk and the challenge as I had nothing to lose and therefore would have no fear about doing the job that needed to be done. So I had accepted the position of hospital administrator of a small community hospital which had been grossly mismanaged for years and the standards of practice, whatever there were of them, were left-over remnants from the dark ages.

The place was knee deep in personal antagonisms, the air thick with skullduggery. Political games were played all over the place. Everyone had their own hidden agenda and if God had made a call for ten just men, even if I could have negotiated Him down to five, we were still done for. The two previous administrators had left under unpleasant circumstances with an average one and a half years' tenure. The atmosphere was so bad that, when the previous administrator's secretary kept insisting on giving me the keys to the hospital car which came with the job, I had been most reluctant to put the key in the ignition in case of a very big bang and flames!

On my second day there I listened to the tape of the summation conference from the recent survey by the Joint Commission on Hospital Accreditation. I didn't know whether I was going to have a stroke or roll over choking on the floor laughing. I had never heard a summation conference that was so bad. I never in my wildest dreams could have imagined such a thing. I couldn't believe that the survey team had even bothered to give a summation of their findings and had not just put a padlock on the front door as they left. I also knew we were not going to get accreditation and that in three months when the decision in head offices in Chicago was to be made, we stood a good chance of closing up unless we could strike a bargain by producing a plan for correcting the deficiencies. If that wasn't bad enough, we had no money and, worse still, we were going into the summer season when patient census was always low. The financial situation was so bleak that the daily delivery men for bread and milk were demanding cash payment at the back door and rumour had it that the dietary department had borrowed two pounds of butter from the nursing home down the hill. Things were not well.

Now even I, who have always loved a challenge and had nothing to lose, paled at the prospects and then I opened a card which had been left on my desk. It was a picture of a huge dragon with a tiny little armoured knight with sword drawn looking up at the beast and challenging him. The caption was "no guts – no glory." Ah! hell I decided to go for it and the story which followed I shall write at some other time because it really was funny, agonizing and totally surreal. To make matters worse, I fell in love with the whole place and the community as well.

I had bomb threats, lawsuits, threatening phone

calls, anonymous letters, my office broken into and my desk rifled, treachery from the most unexpected sources and that was just for starters – in short, a wonderful challenge! However, in the three years I was there, we got a stay of execution from the Joint Commission, built up money in the bank, received an award from President Reagan in the White House. And the local chamber of commerce even gave me a plaque with their Citizen of the Year Award.

But that didn't save me from the political games. I had lasted for three years but, when I sat down to write my letter of resignation on New Year's Day 1989, I had a lovely chuckle to myself. I had stepped on a lot of toes, the owners of which had been sharpening their knives for sometime and were closing in. But those knives were sharpened in vain, I was slipping out from under them just as from the beginning I had known I would.

My timing had been almost perfect but six months earlier would have been better.

On January 2nd 1989 I submitted my letter of resignation and immediately became yesterday's mashed potatoes. This happens when anyone resigns from a controversial position and any expectations to the contrary are totally delusional. Come to think of it I wasn't even sure if the chamber of commerce were going to ask for their plaque back! But it really didn't matter because I had served my time, done what was possible of the job that was needed and was well over the fence and headed for the meadow.

For the first time in twenty-eight years I was unemployed and it felt wonderful. I had the time to organise all the things I needed to do to be ready to leave for Ireland on February 19th. Our plan was to ship everything we wanted to keep from our house and Allan's office along with the new furniture I had bought for the main house. We had decided to put our house up for sale rather than have the bother of renting it out. All electrical appliances we sold and anything else was either given away or went to the Salvation Army.

It is amazing how easy it all was. I just had to tell the movers what to pack and they did it. I made a wonderful haul of pictures and furniture out of Allan's office. His waiting room was furnished with Ethen Allen pieces which I knew would look lovely at Barrow House.

In no time at all everything was done. We had farewell dinners with friends but there was no big deal about leaving them as we would be back in the winter and they would be visiting in the summer. The plan for our first year was to go to Ireland for a few weeks so that I could take care of what needed to be done and then we were off to Europe for six weeks on a Eurail pass. Then we'd go back to Ireland for April in time to meet our sea van shipment and get ready for my first season as an Irish Innkeeper.

Everything really was so easy and well planned and everything on my work list had been done. And then I remembered I had forgotten to buy tickets. Well, that was all right because I had received a special offer in the mail from Delta airlines who were having a special promotion – two first class tickets for the price of one and no advance purchase necessary.

Now I had never flown transatlantic first class before. Business class yes, but never had I even been tempted by the sheer extravagance of a first class transatlantic ticket. But this was a momentous occasion and besides we were getting two tickets for the price of one. Allan got a little pained look on his face but he agreed and I was absolutely delighted.

Now naturally I had to buy a new outfit appropriate to the glamour of my mode of travel. I honestly don't know which I was the most excited about – the glorious future or flying first class. I just couldn't wait. February 19th finally arrived. I dressed in all my finery and we arrived in Atlanta for our flight. I walked into the first class lounge as if to the manor born. I relaxed with my glass of champagne and nibbled on smoked salmon and caviar. Then I strolled through the gate area when the flight was called, ahead of the waiting economy and business class passengers – I mean the Duchess of Windsor couldn't have been more regal than I was. But it would have helped if Allan had dressed up a little and hadn't been carrying a paper bag which contained his newspaper and rolled up jacket!

I sat down in my seat said "Yes, please" to another glass of champagne, glowed in the absolute luxury and promptly fell sound asleep. Allan woke me up for dinner but I couldn't stay awake and I even missed breakfast. I barely had time for a cup of coffee before we had to get off the plane in Shannon. My one and only first class transatlantic travel and I had missed the whole damn thing. I could have been sitting in economy and not have known the difference. There really should have been a refund or something on the price of the ticket.

But the sleep had done me good and I was able to enjoy the excitement and anticipation of actually being able to drive down the driveway of Barrow House and know that I could stay there forever if I wanted to. I was also excited about showing Allan how the place looked now. He hadn't been with me on my last visit and had no idea how beautiful it had turned out to be, yellow door and all. Unfortunately, just when we got outside of Tralee, the rain came lashing down. By the time we got to Barrow we were lucky to be able to see the driveway in front of us, let alone the house and grounds.

We grabbed a few bags and dashed through the rain to our Boathouse apartment which was lovely and warm and cosy.

We had made it, we were home in our little nest in the west and I was going to sit forever looking out the window at whatever I could see of the mountains and bay. It was mine, mine forever and I was going to feast my eyes every second I possibly could. Actually I fell asleep again and didn't wake up for twelve hours!

The following morning the rain stopped long

enough for the sun to come peeping out. I walked to the top of the driveway and started back down slowly enjoying every moment. It didn't matter a bit that my meadow was dripping wet because spring and the bluebells and butterflies would arrive before long. I had all the time in the world.

And as I walked and looked around I became so euphoric at the glorious view of the mountains and bay and the beautiful house with the yellow door that I did something I had never allowed myself to do before – I questioned what I had done with my life. I looked at the peace and loveliness and before I could stop myself I was thinking out loud and asking, "Why didn't I do this sooner – why in the world did I spend my life taking responsibility and punishing myself – what in the hell did I do it for?" And you know something, the answer came flashing through in less than a second. "To pay for this hummer, darlin' – to pay for it." But the payment hadn't just been in dollars. In fact the dollars had probably been the least of the portion – the total payment had been comprised of many things which in the long run meant the nuns had not lied to me one bit!

PART II

TALES OF THE MEADOW

CHAPTER TEN

THE MEADOW

For the first time in our marriage, Allan and I were going to be together twenty-four hours a day, seven days a week and so on ad infinitum. I had heard a lot of women express sheer horror at the thought of their husband's retirement as then he would be under foot all the time. Allan and I had considered this and decided it really wouldn't be a problem as there was so much space and so many things to do at Barrow House that our separate interests would keep us occupied and away from each others' throats.

As for travelling together in the winter time, well, that was going to be easy enough as we were convinced we were both interested in the same things to see and do. We were also positive we would have a wonderful time together sharing the excitement of new places and new experiences. However, there were a few little things we neglected to take into consideration — and one of them was our different reactions to weather.

Yes, we knew that Allan liked hot weather and that I hated it unless I was by a swimming pool with lots of shade and that I liked winter time with a roaring fire, the wind howling outside and being able to feel nice and cosy curled up with a good book or the newspaper. But Allan had always made sure he lived in warm climates. While he thought he could briefly tolerate slightly less favourable weather, he simply was not prepared for February in Ireland.

The first week in our cosy little boathouse apartment was just wonderful. We snuggled up together, read books, opened bottles of good wine, grilled steaks, had candlelight dinners and laughed like school kids having a pyjama party, while the wind howled and the rain lashed against the windows.

Well, that was the first week – the second week with the wind howling and the rain lashing was not quite so much fun. Allan started to get a little wild eyed and took to pacing up and down the hallway. If he had been able to take a walk he would have been fine, but the winds were gales gusting up to sixty miles per hour and the rain kept coming in torrential bursts and that was in between a steady downpour.

Allan started to make snide remarks about us needing an ark and progressed to repeating all the jokes he had ever heard about Irish weather. Only, he wasn't laughing. I tried to tease him out of his gloom but it was too late for he had become obsessed with the weather forecast.

He started out with the six pm news on Irish

television, then the nine pm news on the same channel. He even changed channels, which wasn't difficult, as there are only two in Ireland, the catch being that the news on the second channel is in Irish, but that didn't stop him watching the weather map even though he couldn't understand a word.

The obsession progressed. He used our short wave radio to pick up the six am BBC news which included, not just the weather forecast, but warnings for shipping in coastal regions. He hung on every word and when he heard nothing but gloom and doom he became as one demented. We were quickly on an hourly schedule of listening to the radio and snarling at each other in between.

My humour quickly faded with his nasty jokes about Irish weather – nationalism can be truly blind because I started to take every one of his comments as outrageous slurs and insults towards the land of my parents' birth. An attack on Ireland by an outsider and I was honour bound to defend my heritage. Actually I was somewhat constrained as I couldn't throw a pot or pan for fear of breaking a window in the middle of a storm. The only weapon I had was the viciousness of my tongue. But that wasn't very vicious, as my brain was distracted by the constant roaring of the wind and the sound of rain beating on the windows . . .

It definitely was time for the Eurail Pass.

We kissed and made up, packed our bags and headed for the train station in Tralee, where we would depart for Rosslare to take the ferry to Cherbourg.

Not to return to Ireland until late March, when spring would be in bloom or so I hoped! I had not done any of the things I had planned to do in Ireland before our continental trip but it really didn't matter as there would be time enough when we got back.

When we boarded the ferry at Rosslare, I was still smarting a little from Allan's totally insensitive remarks about Irish weather. Even though I loved my husband dearly, I was just a little smug to discover that Commander Allan Erde, Career Officer, United States Navy, Ret – ex-Medical Officer Pacific Sub Pac Fleet – *got seasick*. Not only that – it was raining like hell when we got to Cherbourg and I loved it. He could rant and rave all about France but he could just leave Ireland alone.

We did our trip through France, Spain and Portugal riding trains, eating and sleeping in wonderfully different places and discovering that we weren't necessarily interested in the same things at all. Well we were, but not exactly to the same degree. Allan likes to walk – I like to walk but if I was going to hoof it over three countries, I hardly saw the need for a Eurail Pass. I wanted to eat in quaint restaurants and enjoy the ambiance. Allan wanted to eat and get out quickly to walk to all the points of tourist interest or just have another little five mile stroll before bedtime. He also knew no fear and wanted to walk down alley ways where I wouldn't have gone in a Sherman tank with an F16 hovering above for air support.

We also had a little difficulty with clothes. I couldn't resist buying some more here and there which made my luggage heavier and heavier to carry. Allan kept complaining. And I complained because Allan was dressing more and more like a down and out. I knew Allan was a little strange about clothes when I married him but we lived in Florida where very casual was acceptable and besides I could throw the worst of his stuff out in the trash when he wasn't looking. It's not that he had terrible taste and style – hell, he didn't have any at all. Terrible would have been an improvement. Worse still, he never threw anything away regardless of the age or condition.

When we had first got married, he had had to clear out a closet of his old clothes so that I would have room for mine. I am being absolutely serious when I confess that I had checked the pockets of everything before he took the lot off to the Salvation Army bin just in case there might be some identification and they would deliver the whole lot back to us.

I already knew all this but we were travelling for six weeks and he had packed his own suitcase. Actually he hadn't packed a suitcase at all – he had had his own dream of the meadow and had bought a backpack along with his Fordor Guide to Europe. The backpack compounded the problem because his clothes got grungier each day and they were travelling rolled up in a ball!

At times I was tempted to pretend I wasn't with him. When we were checking into hotels and I had to admit I really was with him, I was quick to show our passports so the room clerk wouldn't think I was a desperate middleaged lady with a penchant for picking up vagrants!

Our conflict with clothes was aggravating but really was nothing I was not going to be able to overcome if I just gave it a little thought. After all, I reasoned, Allan had a right to play in the meadow too.

I hadn't realised that the two weeks of Irish weather in our lovely little boathouse apartment had seriously brain-damaged Allan on a permanent basis – he really had become obsessed with the weather. It didn't matter what country we were in, the language that was spoken or how late the hour when we arrived in our hotel room – he always turned on the television set and waited for the weather map to see where the bloody jet stream was. He would haunt the news stands of any train station for the arrival of the International Herald Tribune – it wasn't the news, the stock market average or the Nikkei Index he was looking for – hell, it was the damn weather report!

This may all sound as though we didn't enjoy ourselves but we did. We may have had a few grim days such as the one in Antibes, where we didn't speak to each other for eight hours, and the last day in Paris, when we ended up paying one hundred and sixty five pounds for a hotel room because Allan misread the train schedule as well as the hotel tariff listing. Oh and yes, there was the day in Lisbon when he asked me to order lunch for him while he went to the men's room.

He had said he wanted fish and I had a little language difficulty with the waiter, so Allan ended up with octopus in some kind of sauce. Actually it would all have worked out fine if I hadn't told him afterwards what it was he had eaten!

But all in all we laughed and enjoyed each other's company and we both knew that it was just the beginning of the adventure of playing in the meadow. We didn't have to wake up each day and think, "Oh God, what's happened at the office?" or have regrets that there were only a few days left to play before the piper had to be paid! The end of this trip was not an end at all – it was just a stepping stone to the next adventure and the next adventure for me was to go back to Ireland and Barrow House, to start in to the unknown as an Irish Innkeeper. And for Allan – well it was to go back to Ireland and to step into the *completely* unknown world of retirement, married to an Irish Innkeeper, in what would be for him a foreign country with wind and rain, strange accents, strange food, strange surroundings but lots of excitement to look forward to. There was no doubt about it, we both had lots of excitement ahead, but then, who on earth would want their meadow to be boring?

We had a surprise when we got to the ferry in Cherbourg. There were no cabins available. The majority of our fellow passengers were Irish school children returning from an educational trip to France and the organisers had block booked every bunk there was. I was horrified because I knew Allan was going to be seasick and would need to lie down. However, a group of teachers, who were sitting next to us in the restaurant, offered us one of the cabins without our even hinting at it.

We were delighted, but just before we could enjoy our good fortune and go off to bed for the night, we came across an elderly Australian couple who were obviously in more need than we were. We worked out an agreement with them that they would sleep the night in the cabin and then we would take it over in the morning. They protested a little but obviously were too tired and seasick to mean it. It all worked out just fine and Allan only prayed for death a few times before I was able to tuck him up in bed the next morning.

Before we landed in Rosslare we had a chance to get to know our Australians a little better. Win and Harold were from Adelaide and had been retired for some time. They were on their third trip around the world and they had decided this would be the last really big trip. They wanted to take in all the countries which they regretted not having been to before and Ireland was top of their list. They only had four days before they had to be in London and when they named off all the places they wanted to see, using the Eurail Pass, Allan and I just looked at each other.

There was nothing for it but to bring them home with us as they couldn't see the Ring of Kerry, Dingle and the Lakes of Killarney on a train pass in four days. And it was a bank holiday week-end to boot. We decided to put them in the spare bedroom in the boathouse and Allan volunteered to spend the next few days driving them around.

That was our plan but when we got to Rosslare, spring had not sprung in Ireland – it was grey and raining like hell. All across Ireland on the train it rained and we could have been in outer Mongolia for all that we could see out of the window. I was so grateful we had Win and Harold with us because they were such interesting people, their conversation helped to distract Allan from becoming too alarmed at the weather. However, when we had to change trains at Limerick Junction and were waiting on the station platform, Allan did it – yes, he pulled out the short wave radio from his backpack and listened to the weather report including the dangerous shipping warnings for all coastal regions.

As it turned out it was the condition in our own coastal region of Kerry that maybe should have had a little greater emphasis while we still had a chance to beat it back to Europe. We arrived in Tralee in gale force winds. Trees were leaning on the ground and the lamp-posts also. Our caretaker met us with the car and the news that all was not well at Barrow House – well it wasn't the house that had the problem – the house was fine according to Tom – it was getting to it that was going to be difficult as the storms had collapsed the sea wall and part of the driveway was missing. In fact a very large part of the driveway was missing, but he explained that if we parked the car up on the road we would be able to make it down all right if we were careful, as the tide was out!

We helped Win and Harold walk down the long driveway, or what had once been a long driveway, and Allan made a number of trips to carry all the luggage. Tom had been right about the tide because if it had been in full, or even halfway in, we would have been washed out to sea and later been found bobbing in the water somewhere around the Statue of Liberty in New York. No, not only had spring not sprung in Ireland but the weather conditions were many, many times worse than when we had left.

We had barely settled in with everyone's luggage in their bedrooms and the kettle on for tea, hot whiskeys or hemlock as the choice was up for grabs, when the phone rang. It was Auntie Frank.

She wanted to know when we had got back, how we had enjoyed ourselves, had it all been expensive and then with her lovely "gotcha" chuckle she asked, "And how is Allan enjoying our Irish weather?"

Naturally I lied like a dog. She would have expected nothing less where pride or challenge was involved. I cut my response short of implying that he was ecstatically running around the grounds in his shorts exposed to the elements, getting fresh air on his body and loving every minute of it! Mercifully the telephone connection was very bad and the crackling on the line from the storm was such, that if she ever had compared stories with Allan at a later date I could have stone-walled my innocence.

Thirty minutes later our telephone line went out at about the same time as our electricity so we all went to bed with lots of blankets and stayed there until the next morning. The electricity came back on at around nine am but the telephone wasn't to make a sound for another week and a half.

I was worried that Win and Harold would think their Irish trip was a disaster but they were absolutely delighted with everything. They were so grateful as though they thought we had put on the storm and the sea wall disaster especially for them. Allan took them into Tralee when he went grocery shopping and they couldn't have been more delighted than if they had just had a guided tour of Paris with the Louvre thrown in. They loved Tralee which is not surprising, as I think it is a lovely town with lots of character – but in the rain?

We finally had to part company with our delightful new Aussie friends. The day before they had to leave for England, we took them to Killarney and found them a hotel close to the train station as the train left very early in the morning. When we got home, even more of the driveway was missing and the electricity was out again.

Because it was a long holiday weekend and I had no telephone, I hadn't been able to contact anyone to fix the driveway. I was afraid that by the time my builder and his crew arrived there wouldn't be any driveway left to fix and with each crashing tide coming in, it looked more and more as though I was going to be right.

Finally, my builder arrived and gave me an estimate. There really wasn't much point as I certainly was in no position to haggle over the cost. Well, sea walls and driveways don't come cheap, least of all in Ireland, and within a week I was six thousand pounds poorer. But at least we could drive down to the house and, to tell the truth, I wouldn't have complained if the bill had been higher.

A few days later I actually got my telephone line fixed and, with driveway and phone working, things were really looking up. And then one day it happened – I woke up one morning and it was deathly quiet. I jumped out of bed because I just knew something was wrong. I looked out the window and there before me was the most beautiful sight – the sun was coming up and shining over the mountains. Hell, I hadn't seen the mountains in weeks through the rain. There was no rain. It had stopped. There was no sound because the wind was gone and there on the branches of a tree by the window were buds about to leaf. Spring had finally come to Ireland and there it was, magical and beautiful beyond belief, right outside my window.

I yelled to wake Allan to let him know that there was hope after all. But even though he admitted everything looked promising, he turned on the radio for the forecast!

CHAPTER ELEVEN

WORKING THE MEADOW

It was time to get busy. I had a mile long list of things to do. The first priority was to establish a business account at the bank. We already had a personal account but it was time to separate the funds. Allan insisted that I open the business account in another bank so there would be less chance of confusion. That seemed like a good idea, but I did feel a little bit like a traitor to Mike Lynch, the manager of the TSB who had always been so accommodating when I had to deal long distance.

I justified the deed by going to the Bank of Ireland in Tralee. It had been the New York branch which had originally lent me the money to buy Barrow House. When we told the clerk there what we wanted, he went and got someone else who told us we couldn't open a business account unless we had our company approved by the Irish government. When we asked how we did this, he very kindly explained that we couldn't get an approval from the government unless we had a business account!

Obviously we were in the wrong place so we decided to get an accountant. That was next on the things to do list anyway. We went to Frank Stephenson's office on the off-chance that he would be free to see us or, if not, we were going to make an appointment for later. Well, as it happened Frank was available and whoever had recommended him to us in the first place certainly knew their onions.

He listened to our story of what we needed and what we were planning to do. Minutes and one phone call later, we were seated in Rupert Swan's office of the Castle Street branch of Allied Irish Banks and in another few minutes we had a bank account. Then we went back to Frank's office and after another phone call and another few minutes, we had met Joe Murphy, an insurance broker who had just the right guesthouse policy I needed. We liked him so much, we made arrangements to transfer all our insurance coverage to him.

All this in less than an hour. We were delighted with the professional calibre of the three most important people I would need to depend on to start a guesthouse in Ireland. Not only that, but darned if they weren't handsome with wonderful personalities as well – I mean how lucky could I get? Business may be business but it is more fun to deal with people you really like and I had three of them in less than an hour. God was smiling on me. The rain, the sea wall, the driveway and the six thousand pounds became insignificant memories in the past. It was spring in Ireland and I was making progress.

The next item on the agenda was to buy a fax machine. Now this was in 1989 and oddly enough back then fax machines were for some reason uncommon in the USA. So uncommon that I had never seen one. In fact I had never heard of one until I came back to Ireland. When the renovations were going on at Barrow House everyone kept asking me my fax number. I didn't have the faintest idea what they were talking about. Now we were going to buy one so we stopped by an office supply store and they told us they would send their salesman out to Barrow House to demonstrate a machine for us. He arrived the next morning with a brand new fax machine under his arm – in fact it was so brand new he had no idea how it worked. But we got out the instruction book together and tried to figure it out. The salesman was very embarrassed. His company had just switched to that particular machine and this was the first time he was demonstrating it. He was a very nice young man and the sweat kept breaking on his forehead, so we went ahead and bought it anyway even though we still didn't have a clue how to work it.

It took us several days to crack the code of the instruction booklet and when we finally did, it hit me that the Japanese may be excellent at producing good quality items but they really should employ westerners to write the accompanying instructions. The machine was in fact as simple as pie to operate – it was the instructions which were impossible to follow.

Another little surprise the machine held for us was, it cost fifteen hundred pounds including tax but the identical machine which we bought for Kay Rocker in the USA, who would be handling reservations that end, only cost eight hundred dollars! The huge discrepancies in prices between Ireland and anywhere else always make me wonder, who gets the money and how do they get away with it?

My contractor was finishing up the inside of the house, the odds and ends of mantelpieces, closets, shelves and touch up painting. I had an accountant, banker and insurance agent and a fax machine that worked. All I needed, apart from an obscure relative to die and leave me lots of money, was an employee to work with me at Barrow House.

Well, actually I already had my co-worker lined up, I was just waiting for her to get back from a trip to America. I had lucked out on a previous visit to Ireland and had met a distant cousin whose older sister and I used to play together years ago when we were young. I hadn't remembered Ina from those days as she would have been too small but it was a blessing from heaven to have found her now.

If you can imagine an attractive lady in her late forties with outrageous humour, incredible generosity, true warmth, complete zest for life – and a complete rogue – then you have just a small insight into my cousin Ina.

Ina does nothing by halves – if she is going to clean house, everything gets moved, dust flies out of every window, and not one corner, nook or cranny is overlooked. If she is going to a party, she is not seen for three days! If anyone asks for her help she will take the shirt off her back, and if that's not enough, she will ransack the neighbourhood. She has the temper of a wounded lion and the gentleness of a lamb. She is a true free spirit, who marches to her own drummer.

In case you can't tell I have true affection and admiration for my wonderful cousin – she also has driven me crazy from time to time, but I doubt if there is a human in this world who could ever stay mad at Ina for over three minutes and she can't stay mad at anyone for over one minute. Ina was my first employee at Barrow House and we shall both vividly remember the experience for the rest of our lives.

We started out in cold April planting hundreds of pansies around the place as there was nothing else we could do until the furniture arrived for the main house. Spring may have sprung and the wind and rain might have gone but it was still colder than hell, especially when the sun disappeared behind the clouds. Allan kept telling us exactly what the temperature was but we ignored his warnings of impending death from hypothermia. After two days of planting neither of us could straighten up or walk without pain. I mean pain. Only hot whiskies and hot baths followed by hot whiskies could ease our bodies in the slightest. But still each day we planted those damn pansies in the bitter cold.

Finally one day we had word that the container van

with all the furniture and other belongings was on the way. That was the good news. The bad news was that the van was twice the width of my driveway, five hundred yards long from the road down to the courtyard in front of Barrow House! I started to panic at the impossibility of unloading everything at the top of the driveway and getting it down to the house when Ina told me not to worry, it would be all be taken care of.

Sure enough the next morning a small truck arrived. Ina, her sons, some neighbours and a crowd of other people I had not met before all collected in the courtyard along with the customs agent who was there to assess the duty on our shipment. The huge truck pulled up at the top of the driveway and we all went up to meet it. The customs agent broke the seal and everyone, except the three delivery men, started to unload its contents into the small truck which would ferry loads up and down the driveway. A group was assigned to load and unload and I was told by Ina to get out of the way and stand by the front door and tell them where everything should go. I stood one side of the door and the customs officer stood the other side, as he totted up the value of everything that went past him.

The whole scene was hilarious. My dedicated crew tried to pull off new price tags and cover over everything that might look expensive, all under the eyes of the customs officer. The three delivery men stood watching the whole thing, looking somewhat like the Irish version of Larry, Mo and Curly. If I had been depending on those gentlemen I think it would have taken ten days. Instead the van was emptied in eight hours including lunch break, and every piece of furniture was in its place. The whole of the US engineers' corps couldn't have done a better job. And to this day I don't know where the little truck came from.

We spent the next few weeks arranging furniture and hanging pictures. When we disagreed about where anything went, I always got my way. Then the next day when I went into the house it would be arranged exactly the way Ina wanted it. This went on for several weeks until we reached a compromise. She could put the plants anywhere she wanted to, but the furniture and pictures were mine. This was fine, but the furniture did continue to move a little.

We finally had the house ready. We stocked the kitchen, polished the floors again and just looked at each other. It was time to go on to the next step – guests. Neither one of us were ready for that moment, so we had cleaned the whole house all over again, watered the pansies and found anything we could to do to put off the inevitable.

After a few days Allan enquired casually if we were ever going to open the guesthouse. I told him it couldn't possibly be done until I had a sign made and that would take at least a week. He came out of his office a few minutes later with a large package, which he presented to me in front of Ina. Oh God, it was a sign for the driveway entrance which read, "Barrow House De-luxe Bed and Breakfast." It was his opening present to me, which he had had specially made. He was delighted with himself and he got out his tool box and went off up the driveway to officially put us in business.

As soon as he left, Ina and I panicked. "What are we going to do? Someone might come down the driveway!"

"What if they don't like the place?"

"What if they are horrible and mess up the place?"

"What if we've forgotten something?"

"What if no one comes down the driveway?"

"Oh God, why did he have to be so helpful?"

"We'd have been fine if we could have just done it in our own time."

"What are we going to do?"

Well there was only one thing to do. We lit the fire in the guest diningroom, opened a bottle of wine and agreed that it really was time to start taking guests. When we finished the bottle of wine, we had the whole thing under control and our courage was back. We reasoned that, after all, it wasn't like a hospital where, if you did something wrong, you could kill someone. We did have to get our feet wet sometime soon as we had scheduled guests coming the following week.

We decided yes, we were ready to open for guests, but we opened another bottle of wine instead and decided that Ina would tie a bed sheet over the sign on her way home. Tomorrow would be soon enough. There was no point in opening at that time of the evening and it would be much better to start with a fresh day – so much for courage!

CHAPTER TWELVE

BARROW HOUSE DE LUXE
BED AND BREAKFAST

The next morning Ina took the sheet off the sign as she came to work and that was it – we were in business. We made sure the cash box had change in it and the new receipt book on my desk had several pens lying next to it. Ina insisted on checking the house to make sure that no dust had fallen on the furniture during the night. The kitchen and dining room floor got polished again and then we heard a car. It turned out to be the postman!

By two o'clock Ina had checked the bed and breakfast sign at the top of the driveway twice to make sure that it had not fallen down. We still hadn't had even a nibble. Then around three o'clock a car came into the driveway with four people in it. We fell on it from either side to make sure it didn't get away. Auntie Frank was absolutely delighted that we had given her and her friends such an enthusiastic welcome, although of course she would have expected nothing less. She had brought out friends for a tour and had not phoned because she had wanted to surprise me – well she did that.

There's no doubt about it, they were impressed. And well they should have been because the house and grounds looked beautiful. Everyone "oohed" and "aahed." Auntie Frank kept saying "Oh Maureen, what a job – how on earth did you get it to look like this? It must have cost a fortune." It hadn't come cheap but I didn't mind at all letting her jump to her own conclusions as to the amount spent. It would pay her back for giving me hell over that new bungalow she had wanted me to buy. Besides it would give her more pleasure bragging with pride to the neighbours if she wasn't tied down to exact amounts.

Auntie Frank and her friends very definitely made us feel very good. I laughed again when she asked me the usual question about Allan. "Whatever did you do to deserve him? You've got the luck of the devil."

I didn't tell her that her special little pet was over in the boathouse listening to the weather forecast and thinking up something nasty to say about Irish weather. But if I had done, she would probably have sided with him anyway. Auntie Frank also asked us where all the guests were but we brushed it off with a vague explanation that they weren't expected until the next week.

When the group left it was time for Ina to go home and still we didn't have a guest but at least we'd had a pleasant distraction to keep us from listening for the sound of tyres on the driveway.

I walked with Ina to the courtyard and, just as I thought she was leaving she suddenly turned and said, "I just thought of something." To my surprise she went running up the steps into the big house.

When she came back I asked her, "What was that about?"

She explained with a grin, "Oh I just turned on all the lights in the front rooms of the house – all the neighbours know we're open and they're watching, so let them think we're full!" I loved it. Only Ina could have come up with an idea like that.

For the next few days we continued to wait and wait for that first drop-in guest but all we got were drop-in sightseers. Lord only knows where they all came from but we gave our tours and everyone "oohed" and "aahed" and asked how many guests we had and we nonchalantly explained that they wouldn't arrive until the following week, as though there was not a thought in our heads that anyone was expected sooner.

Our first group of four arrived as scheduled for two days. We tried to act as if we did this all the time but every possible thing went wrong. I forgot to turn on the hot water for their suite, Ina burnt the breakfast bacon three times and I forgot to buy bread for toast. We were off to a great start, but we overcame these little problems without batting an eye. Ina opened the kitchen window to let out the smoke and I climbed out, ran over to our boathouse apartment, stole Allan's loaf of bread and climbed back in the window.

We did this quite often when we ran out of things we needed. Ina was responsible for breakfast and, if she needed something, she would just buzz me on the intercom. I would run over in my night-gown and either climb in my office window, or throw it in the kitchen window. We did this so that I didn't have to walk through the guest dining room and make it obvious that supplies were not what they should be in the kitchen, and besides, I was still in my night-shirt!

When our first guests left they were delighted with their stay, and every year I have someone make a reservation because of their recommendation. Robert O'Malley of Denver, Colorado, I love you!

Our next guests were not due until the end of the month as our reservations were few and far between that first year. So the time had come to get bolder and put up another "Bed and Breakfast" sign, to attract business from the road. All golfers going to the Tralee Golf Club have to pass Barrow House, so with a little bit of luck they would respond to our signs.

We put up the sign and again waited . . . and waited . . . Two days later we got our first nibble. But they didn't stay as they were only looking for a place to stay next year! More and more people dropped in out of curiosity and finally some stayed. The phone had started ringing with reservations and we really were in business.

That's when we found out one of the six chimneys

was totally blocked up. Ina lit the fire in one of the suites in preparation for a guest arrival, and smoke went everywhere. Now when Ina lights a fire there is nothing meagre about it – if you want to smelt steel, just use one of Ina's fires. It took us forever to get the damn thing out, and we were choked and black from the smoke.

I called a chimney sweep out from town, and he got huge boxes of twigs and ancient crow nests down, but the chimney was still blocked at the top where his equipment could not reach. As you already know, Barrow House was built in 1723 and has four floors including the semi-basement area. The chimney that was blocked started on the ground floor, so it travelled a heck of a long way to the top of the chimney pot. There was nothing for it but to get a hoist from town and clear out the chimney from the top. This operation was successful but it also cost all the income made from guest receipts to that point. I was starting to get the message that an innkeeper's life can be very exciting – and expensive. But I looked on the bright side: at least the chimney was clean!

A few days later we heard screams from the house. Ina and I almost knocked each other down to get there. One of our guests was yelling hysterically in the hallway that a big black bird was flying around the sitting room of her suite. Yes, it was the same damn suite and the crows had been so used to landing in safety that they were now falling down the chimney – God help us.

We calmed the guest down with a sup of brandy which we naturally shared as our nerves were shot from her screams and from having to catch the crow. By the time her husband returned from playing golf she was totally mellowed out and thought the whole thing delightfully funny. We laced him with brandy, just to be sure that he also thought it delightfully funny. Brandy is very expensive in Ireland and there went the profits from their two-day stay. Oh well, we did eventually have a good laugh – a little hysterical but laughter just the same!

After that we had to establish a crow check in the house and a gun squad outside. Gerald Landers, who is a crack shot, came every evening for four days and eliminated enough of them so that the crow emergency was over for the time being.

That first year I had decided that, rather than spend a lot of money on advertising, I would just include free dinner as an opening special. My time was expendable, and I love to cook. So Ina cooked breakfast, and took care of the house, and I did the reservations, correspondence, the shopping and cooked dinner. We both had to clean up after ourselves, but Allan helped me in the evening.

I have found that the part of being an innkeeper which I enjoy the most, apart from collecting the money, is the evening meal. I love to cook with Irish food, as it is of such good quality. I also like to fix food that is traditionally associated with Ireland, such as Irish stew, roast lamb and shellfish. Boiled bacon and cabbage is on the menu, but I have now cooked it so many times by popular request that the smell of it makes me nauseous, and my gall bladder cringes just at the thought of the stuff. However it is still on the menu, and my guests love it.

It's not just the preparation of the evening meal which I enjoy, it's actually getting to know the guests. After dinner over coffee is when I really enjoy their conversation. I never cease to be amazed at how interesting people are. Everyone has a story which is uniquely their own. Listening to them is a privilege and a profound lesson in the sheer goodness and resilience of the human race. I've had a few bastards too, but that is rare enough.

It was just as well that I was fixing meals such as Irish stew and bacon and cabbage, because it was a "freebie" and I had to keep costs under control. The one thing I hadn't thought of was guests wanting wine with their dinner. I did not have a wine licence because I had been wrongly informed that it would cost me six thousand pounds. Now good wine in Ireland is incredibly expensive, and bad wine is not much cheaper. There was, as Ina explained it, only one option. We would have to serve homemade wine.

I explained to her that I had never made wine, and she just shrugged her shoulders and said, "Nothing to it, you just buy a kit in town and I'll make it." Well, I bought the kits, one white, one red, and Ina made up a few gallons of something that looked a little suspicious, but obviously she knew what she was doing. She tended to the brew every day, and consulted the directions on the package. Every so many days she would filter it and have me taste it. She insisted that I knew more about wine than she did. I did this with increasing reluctance as the stuff tasted awful!

Then after it had aged for a full three weeks and filtered for the final time, as per the instructions, she made me taste it one more time. God, it was awful! The white was so sweet that I gagged, and the red was so coarse and bitter my mouth puckered and my throat went on fire. Ina suggested that, since we had nothing to lose, we should dump the two together and when I tasted the results, I said it was one of the most delicious wines I had ever tasted. She was so delighted that she told me she had never made wine before in her life! And I immediately visualised my liver with holes in it!

As luck would have it, we had two sisters from California as guests, one of whom came down to the dining room while I was choking and waiting to go blind. It turned out that she was a wine buyer for a huge supermarket chain, and she volunteered to sample our brew. I cannot say how intensely relieved I was when she pronounced it excellent. No wonder I'm an optimist and believe that God works in mysterious ways, His wonders to behold. If Ina had just remembered how she had done it, we would have had spectacular wine for the season. She didn't but she did come up with a reasonable facsimile. I am not sure of the legal ramifications. It's possible we could have been considered to be making "moonshine." However, our guests loved it, we didn't charge for it and Bord Fáilte should be proud of us as we made friends for Ireland!

And where was Allan during all the hustle, bustle and hidden chaos and confusion of Ina and I opening the guesthouse? Well he was right in there creating the chaos and confusion for us to overcome.

To begin with, Allan spent most of his time reading, basking in the sun, taking long walks, gathering travel brochures for winter and announcing all weather news including the location of the jet stream to anyone he could find to listen.

Every so often he violated our agreement and started to tell me how to run Barrow House. But I turned on him spitting like a jungle cat and he backed off quickly. Then he tried a different approach and announced that I had totally misunderstood his previous efforts. All he wanted to do was help me, he wanted an assignment.

I was a little leery of this. Allan had already mown down all my young sunflowers and growing corn stalks when he ventured to mow the back lawn. But it did seem reasonable enough that he would want something to do around the place so I gave him the peat briquette assignment. He was to pick up enough bales of briquettes every week for the six fireplaces in the house and put them in every suite.

It was still early in the summer and although we

were not that busy it was a chore to remember to buy the briquettes at our village store and load the bales in the trunk of my car, not to mention hauling them out again and up the stairs to the suites. Yes, Ina and I thought it was very nice that Allan had volunteered.

About two days later after breakfast when a goodly group of guests had paid their bill, I did some rough mathematics and was delighted to announce to Ina that the operating budget was actually in the black by almost eight pounds. Our chorus of cries of success were interrupted by a loud rumbling noise outside. When I went to check what it was I found a large flatbed truck out in the courtyard turning around to park by the diningroom door. Two men got out and asked me where I wanted the briquettes – I pointed to the spot where we usually kept the six bales and thought how silly it was of Allan to have this huge truck come down the driveway for such a small delivery. But it wasn't a small delivery! Thirty minutes later the driver knocked on the kitchen door and presented me with a bill for one hundred and fifty three pounds. All I could see were bales of briquettes everywhere – one hundred and twenty six bales to be precise – I wrote the cheque in stunned silence.

Ina, who had been totally unaware of the delivery truck, kept asking me what was the matter and all I could say was "Wuh-wuh-wuh-wun hundred and fuh-fuh-fuh – I'll kih-kih-kih-kill him!"

I should have known what he would have done

with that assignment – I had been married to him long enough. When I first married him and moved into his house, there had been fifty-six tins of enchiladas, forty tins of refried beans and ten extra large economy containers of washing-up liquid in his kitchen, at least one hundred bars of soap and twenty-four tins of spray deodorant in his bathroom, and the spare room was stocked wall to wall with toilet rolls and paper towels. And worse, when I later had told him the price of the tombstone for my grandparent's grave, he said, "Darling, why on earth didn't you buy two?"

Well there I was in the red again but when I calmed down we had another good laugh. But then we had to move the huge stack of briquettes so the guests would be able to get in the dining-room door for dinner. We looked like coal miners when we were through. Allan was a wise man and had disappeared when he heard me roaring over the bill. He lay low for a few days, taking long walks and trips to the library and not even suggesting that he wanted to be helpful. Then one evening he came over to the guest kitchen just as dinner was about to be served. There were eight guests and I had all the plates set out on the kitchen counter while I was putting the food on them. Mary, who helped me in the kitchen in the evenings, and I had a routine. She would pull the hot plates from the oven and I would put portions on them. She would then serve four plates to the guests while I was preparing the remainder, so they would be ready to go out to the diningroom as soon as she returned and still be nice and hot.

Well that evening Allan wanted to "help" so I said "ok." Before I could turn around he had disappeared with two plates, and I had no idea whether they had food on them or not. I had to get Mary to run after him and get the plates back. They had already been served to guests with just potatoes on them. When he saw the plates being picked up he went out and grabbed two from under guests' noses that were perfectly all right. I had to send him back to return them. When everyone was served and things had settled down in the kitchen, Allan went out to the diningroom to gather up the empty plates long before anyone could possibly have been finished eating their meal. When I realised what he was doing I was going to stop him but as I got to the dining-room door I heard him say, "Well I hope you enjoyed your dinner and I also hope everyone got their own plates back in all that shuffle!" Dessert was already laid out in the kitchen so I just went down the hall to my office and climbed out the window into the night!

Well, that was the first time I fired Allan as a waiter. If I'd had any sense I wouldn't have had to fire him a second time. Allan doesn't drink alcohol of any kind, not because he is noble or has religious convictions, but because he is truly allergic to the stuff and even dessert liquor on ice cream would put him on a respirator in intensive care. This may seem as though fate played him a cruel hand but actually I see it more as mercy from above as the jokes he tells are bad enough without the effects of alcohol to enhance them. However, it doesn't bother him a bit to be around people who are drinking unless, of course, they are belligerently drunk. For the most part he enjoys people who have imbibed because they laugh harder at his jokes. In Florida we would go out to dinner to the same restaurant every Monday night with our friends Bill and Janie Carson. The three of us always drank wine while Allan had his coffee and somehow over the years we developed a joke about winos and caffeine freaks – well it may not sound funny now but it's one of those things where you had to have been there.

One evening, after Allan had long been banished from the diningroom and kitchen, he came over looking particularly lonely and pathetic and asked if he could "help". There really wasn't anything to do but foolishly I told him he could check and see if anyone would like more wine, after all it was homemade and hardly cost anything. He was obviously delighted to get another chance and picked up a chilled carafe of wine, walked into the diningroom and announced, "Okay, which of you winos would like another glass?"

I wanted to climb out the window – actually I could have crashed out the window without waiting to open it, but instead I had to bounce into the diningroom and start laughing and talking and pouring wine to cover Allan's incredible faux pas and do something about the horrible, chilled silence which he had brought about.

I think I explained something about frontal lobe epilepsy and that sometimes the medication didn't work but it would be all right as I would give him a double dose that night and he'd be better in the morning. I may also have said something about "head injury", "war wound", "purple heart", "sad case" – hell! I was so rattled I don't know what I said. The guests probably went to bed that night hoping I'd take a double dose of medication too!

CHAPTER THIRTEEN

THE ABBEYFEALE CAPER

About the middle of that first summer, Ina decided that she needed a car, but she didn't have any money. Not being one to let a little detail like that get her down, she went to an old family friend in Abbeyfeale, who had a used car lot, and picked out one, with the promise of payment later. When she drove it into the courtyard the next day, I was totally amazed that it had made the journey from Abbeyfeale, which is about thirty miles away. The tyres were bald, the engine was in agony, and the passenger door was tied shut, and those were the best parts! The chassis looked as if it had been hit in all directions by a bulldozer, and it was impossible to determine what had been the original colour. But Ina rolled down the window, opened the car door with the outside handle and climbed out, pleased as punch, while I stood there with my mouth open.

She had already named this wreck "Daisy." On the way back from Tralee with her little niece in the passenger's seat, she had said "Whoopsa Daisy" every time they hit a bump in the road, as the car had no shocks. The agreed price for this magnificent bundle of twisted metal was five hundred pounds. So much for an old family friend! Now Ina is nobody's fool, and all she wanted was transportation, and she hoped with a little time she could drive the price down.

After a few months of negotiations on the telephone, the seller still would not budge on the price. So she went to plan B, and came up with a brilliant idea.

The two of us would go to Abbeyfeale, and phone the used car salesman to ask him to meet us in a pub. We would put some drinks down him, and then I was to lay down three hundred pounds cash on the bar, and tell this guy I was buying the car for Ina, but that was all I was willing to pay. He could take his choice. Three hundred pounds now or chase Ina the rest of his life for five hundred pounds. Then I was to put in the hook by saying he had fifteen minutes to make up his mind!

Well we did it – we drove to Abbeyfeale that very afternoon, went to the pub, downed a drink for courage, and made the call. Just before our man arrived, Ina changed the game plan to two hundred pounds, so I put the other one hundred pounds in my coat pocket just in case.

Dave, our used car salesman, arrived and insisted on buying us a drink, so we drank it. Then, feeling a little guilty about what we were about to do, I bought a round of drinks, and we drank them. Then Ina, feeling either a little twinge, or wanting to go for the kill, ordered another round, and we drank that. Now it was time for me to perform.

I put the two hundred pounds on the counter and went through my rehearsed speech as best I could remember it, considering the alcohol imbibed. I paused and watched for a response. He looked at the cash on the counter, then at each of our faces, then at the clock on the wall, then back at the cash on the counter. This was a man in true agony – not because of the money, but because he knew we had him. What a terrible fate for a used car salesman! However, I will say this, he had class – he reached over, picked up the money without saying a word, put it in his pocket, and called for another round. Never in my life did I think I would help to best a used car salesman. And here I was, with the scene right in front of me, and I was intoxicated in more ways than one!

It was six o'clock in the evening when we left Abbeyfeale, and I realised that Allan would be wondering where I was. We stopped at a pay phone to call him, but it was out of order, so Ina said not to worry, we would stop in Castleisland and make the call.

We stopped in Castleisland, but it wasn't at a phone box, it was at the Crown. I went to use the phone at the rear of the bar, and, when I came back, everyone was talking to Ina, and there were two drinks on the counter for me. Well, this was the evening of our success, and it seemed quite appropriate that we enjoy it. I also realised that it was not possible to go anywhere in Ireland where Ina did not have friends delighted to see her and buy her drinks.

We left Castleisland. By this time I was feeling no pain, and on our way into Tralee I decided that we should stop into the Ballygarry House Hotel to say hello to Owen McGillicuddy, as it was his lovely place I had brought medical groups to in the past. We had no intention of scrounging a drink, so we sat down and quickly ordered one, and paid for it before I asked if Owen was around. Well, he was, and yes, he insisted on us staying around for another drink on him!

Still euphoric from our success and other things, we left Tralee, and thought we were headed home but, as we got close to the Oyster Tavern at Spa, we realised how hungry we were. By this time it was eight-thirty pm and I knew Allan would have gone ahead and eaten without me.

We pulled into the parking lot in a flash, and, before we could help ourselves, we were seated at a table ordering lobster and my favourite wine. After all, we had saved one hundred pounds on the car transaction. As fate would have it Frank Stephenson, my accountant walked in the door and saw us. The next thing I knew there was another bottle of Mateus Rosé on the table. As fate would further have it, my insurance man and special consultant Joe Murphy walked in the door, and yes, there was another bottle of Rosé on the table.

I should pause here and say that my usual drink is wine, and Irish bar wine is horrible, and the Irish system of ordering rounds is lethal for anyone who wants to cling on to any appearance of sobriety. So after a few sessions where, when it finally came to my turn to buy a round, and I was practically flat out on the bar, I devised a defensive Irish drinking routine. I would buy the first round and make my order a bottle of rosé. This way I could easily pass on drinks when the following rounds were bought, and also leave whenever I wanted to with whatever was left of my bottle of wine.

When Frank Stephenson and Joe Murphy asked the bartender to send over a drink to our table of whatever I drank, they must have had one hell of a shock. But they are such lovely gentlemen that they did it anyway. Fortunately for them, it was the one and only time we ran into each other when out for the evening. Either that or they've seen my car in the parking lot and gone somewhere else!

Needless to say we needed those two bottles of wine like a hole in the head. The food having given me back some semblance of sobriety, faint though it was, I put one under each arm and we headed home. We got to the top of the driveway when Ina remembered the "Stations." I had no idea what she was talking about, so she explained that the parish is divided up into areas, and each family in that area takes turns having Mass said in the house. This is also the time when everyone settles their church dues with the priest. Food and drink is served and the social gathering can turn into quite a party, depending on whose house the Stations are held at. Years ago it was a very big thing, as many families with small children or elderly could not travel the distance to church as frequently as they would have liked. Attending Stations was a religious and social occasion that gave a welcome break from routine for many isolated families.

One of Ina's friends had the Stations that day, and Ina had promised her she would bring me over as I had not yet met her. By this time it was so late that it hardly made any difference what time I got home, so we turned around and off we went.

When we walked into the house we expected to find a party in full swing, but instead everyone went quiet when we entered. My God, everyone looked so prim and proper, and here I was meeting the neighbours for the first time, and me practically legless! I was horrified but I at least I had the presence of mind to sit down quickly and keep my mouth shut.

We left shortly afterwards, but it was still two o'clock in the morning when I got into bed. My husband woke up and asked me where I had been, to be so late, and I told him I was at the "Stations." That really woke him up. He thought I meant the police station! I very sleepily told him that it was a religious thing, that I would explain in the morning, and promptly lost consciousness.

The next morning when I recounted with glee how we had outsmarted a used car salesman, my husband, being a man, and all men seem to stick together, simply smiled and said, "You'd better watch out, paybacks are hell." Talk about sour grapes, but it was a prophecy.

Within a week, Ina's brother and sister-in-law were having the stations and I told Ina that I wasn't up to any more drunken revelry for at least another twenty years. We both agreed that we would go over at four-thirty pm, eat our sandwiches daintily with a cup of tea, and leave like proper, well-behaved, middle-aged matrons. That was what we intended, but this was Ireland. It just didn't work out that way.

When we got there, two of the very prim and proper ladies from the previous Stations were just arriving. We sat down very nicely in the parlour, and Ina, who was very much at home in her brother's house, took over as hostess. She offered them both a drink, and when they demurred, she absolutely insisted and went off to the kitchen to fix them in more ways than one! When she served the drinks she gave me a furtive wink and I knew what it meant. As the contents of their glasses were drained, she hovered solicitously and made sure that their glasses were well tended to. It wasn't long before those ladies relaxed and became quite gregarious. We all got to talking and laughing and they told us how horrified they were when they saw Ina bring me in the door the week before, as they had been tippling all evening, and they were alarmed that I would think they were drunk. They were so concerned about their own condition they never realised how badly off we were!

That's when I put down my cup and saucer and let Ina fix me a drink, just one, as I had to get home! Some more people came in, and there was music and singing and people telling stories and when daylight came, I had to seriously consider going home!

As I climbed into bed, my husband asked me just exactly what was this religious rite, but I was snoring before I could answer.

CHAPTER FOURTEEN

PAYBACKS ARE HELL

Nothing simple happens in Ireland, so it's hard to tell a simple story. Anyway I'll try to explain how we ended up with three dogs. The moral of this tale is, "Never get a free Irish dog from an Irish used car salesman." Take this advice from one who knows!

The whole thing started out simply enough. I was invited by friends to join them for dinner one St Patrick's Day, as I was alone at Barrow House. It was a lovely evening, my hosts grilled steaks, plied me with wine, and then showed me the last puppy left in the litter. They even let me hold him. They told me the puppy had obviously fallen in love with me, and wouldn't it be wonderful for me to take him home. It was a set-up but I fell for it anyway.

The next morning I woke up with a sore head and a little black puppy in a plastic bag next to me. I had at least had the sense to put his lower half in a plastic bag before taking him to bed with me. I had named him Paddy the night before, in honour of St Patrick.

As I lay there looking at him and wondering what I had done, he opened his little eyes and licked my face. Yes, he was mine!

I told my husband on the phone that we had a new addition to the family, and he was so relieved that it was only a puppy that he didn't mind a bit.

Paddy was just a little six week old ball of black fur with big feet, but he had the disconcerting habit of snuggling up to be petted, and then he would sink his teeth into a hand or arm. For a few weeks we thought this was cute and funny, but he was growing rapidly, and he was starting to do serious damage to our persons. My husband and I had hands and arms that made us look like druggies with a serious needle problem.

I went to town and bought a couple of books on the care and training of Labradors. The first one was mostly concerned with diet – it stated that it was very important for Labradors to have high protein meals, with plenty of meat and fish, and that generous servings of green vegetables were also absolutely necessary. Broccoli and green beans were highly recommended! This crazy book went into such detail on meal planning for "your new puppy" that I was surprised they didn't specify what china to serve it on!

The next book was written by someone with a name like Lady Susan Hunter-Brown. Now she went into more detail about training and having the right relationship with your puppy. She stated that

Labradors must never be spanked or spoken harshly to, as they are so sensitive you can create severe psychological damage with one cross word.

I looked down at my hands and arms, and then at my sleeping little ball of black fur, and wondered which of us was suffering psychological damage.

But we spoke softly to our little darling, hid the broccoli in his puppy food, and resisted the instinct to whack the little bastard when he sank his teeth in. Lady Susan Hunter-Browne had obviously never met a little Kerry dog, and the only sensible use for the book would have been to brain the little cannibal with it. Actually, it was very frustrating as he really was very loving, except when he was biting, and the only thing that stopped us from throttling him was that we loved him dearly. Somehow we knew he just didn't mean to hurt us.

I had to find an answer to the problem. I could hardly have a guesthouse with a family dog which savaged the guests. We couldn't get rid of him, we had all fallen in love with him. Ina would put his baby blue blanket by the fire in the dining room after the breakfast guests were gone, and Johnny the postman would give him a piece of his cookie when he stopped for coffee. Johnny wanted to know if we had bought Paddy a fishing rod yet, but I had to tell him that Paddy was far too young for that.

We then had some guests who had raised many of their own hunting dogs, and I told them about my problem. Marie and Wally from Roscrea said there wasn't a problem – bring Paddy out, and Wally would show me how to handle him. I put my little ball of black fur into Wally's arms, and after a little petting, sure enough, he started to bite him. Wally said "watch me", and he raised his forefinger and tapped Paddy firmly against the side of his nose. If Paddy's mouth and teeth had been bigger, Wally's arm would have been gone. So much for that lesson, but Wally and Marie have become our good friends, although Wally has treated Paddy cautiously ever since!

I finally decided that since Paddy really didn't realise he was hurting us, the only solution was to do exactly what you do with little kids who bite – you bite them back, to show it hurts!

There was no way that I was going to risk my face by biting him, so we'd have to get another puppy, and let it be a peer group learning situation! This seemed really a good idea. Also when we were gone in the winter and Paddy was left here with the caretaker, he would have a little friend to play with. I mentioned this casually to Ina and said that I would really like the new puppy also to be a male black Labrador, and the same age as Paddy. I knew it would take me a while to find one with those requirements, but I forgot that this was Ireland!

Well, strangely enough, within two days Ina told me that her brother had told her he knew of one that met my exact requirements. The owner was willing to give him away just to be sure that the pup would have a good home. I was delighted, and asked where this pup was. When she said Abbeyfeale, I should have instantly said "No." When she said, "Dave, the used car salesman" I should have emigrated, but when she said, "He is a beautiful little pup and he is going to get a bullet in his head if nobody takes him", I said "Let's go!"

We got to Abbeyfeale about ten-thirty on a Saturday morning. When we arrived at Dave's house, we had to step over bodies in sleeping bags on the floor. They'd had a huge twenty-first birthday party the night before, and many of the guests had stayed overnight. I was anxious to meet my puppy, but Dave insisted that we have a drink – we said no but it was perfectly obvious that if we didn't have a drink, I wasn't going to get the puppy, so we had the drink.

Then we went to the bottom of the garden where he kept his hunting dogs, and out of the pen he brought this gorgeous black pup, and put him in my arms. The pup immediately put his paws around my neck and snuggled his face to the side of mine – he had found his owner. Actually from what I know now, he was probably signalling the used car salesman over my shoulder to, "Move out bud, this sucker is mine!"

Dave's daughter came down, saw the puppy in my arms, and said that she wanted it. Now this was the one who had the twenty-first birthday, and her father said, "No, this one is for Maureen." Oh I should have been suspicious, but I think he'd laced my drink and my guard was down!

As we were leaving, Dave asked us to give him a lift to the pub, and of course that meant another drink. Actually it meant several more, as everyone in the small pub wanted to toast my new pup who had been named Séamus by Ina. Séamus sat under my bar stool the whole time we were there, without a whimper or a movement. He was obviously going to be a very good little dog!

An Irish pub is one of the most interesting places in the world. I'm not talking about the tourist ones, although they are a lot of fun also, but the small town pubs, where you go in with a local person, are an absolute delight. The wit and humour is unparalleled and the characters are just brilliant. It's like sitting through your own private Irish version of "Cheers".

And well, yes, it was late in the afternoon when we got home, and Allan said he wasn't the least bit surprised as he had noticed that Abbeyfeale seemed to have that effect on us!

I introduced Paddy to his new brother – they looked each other over, sniffed around and started to play. Paddy must have got carried away and bit too hard, because Séamus womped him good, and Paddy came running over to my chair with a look that said, "Mommy, when's this one going home?" However, they seemed to get on reasonably well, and I made up their little sleeping baskets by the back door. Paddy had never slept outside, as when I first got him it was too cold, and then I was afraid he would be too lonely. But now that he had a little brother, it was obviously time to wean him from the house. I tucked them in, said "goodnight", and went indoors. I was halfway down the hallway when the noise started; I stopped dead in my tracks. The howling sounded like the Hound of the Baskervilles right at my door!

I went back and opened the door, and there was Séamus. He wasn't the size of a teddy bear, but the noise coming out of him would have woken the neighbours for miles around. As I stood there looking at him, he got up and walked past me down the hallway into my bedroom, and lay down on my sheepskin decorator rug. Paddy, obviously delighted, trotted right along behind him and curled up next to Séamus on the rug. Now Séamus had never slept in a house in his life, but had staked a claim to my sheepskin rug. There was no way I could put him outside, or I would have been in front of a judge on neighbourhood disturbance charges. Yes, paybacks are hell, and with Séamus they were only just beginning!

The black dogs are now six years old and, with a few exceptions, have slept in our bedroom ever since. The few exceptions were when we put their sheepskin rugs in the hallway and closed our bedroom door. That worked for a few nights until Séamus learned how to turn the door handle! We put a lock on the inside, but he sat outside scratching the paint off and howling. He also developed another nasty little trick. If he was allowed to sleep in the bedroom at the very beginning he would sleep on his rug until daylight, when he would land in the middle of the bed between us for his morning petting. If, however, he had to go through the effort of demanding entrance he immediately landed in the middle of the bed and insisted on staying there for the night. He gave us a choice, his way or his way!

Paddy is not the slightest bit jealous of Séamus, but Séamus is pathologically jealous of his brother. From the beginning, Séamus wanted all the attention and even resented tennis balls being thrown for Paddy to chase. Séamus would never run for a ball, and let us know right off that it was beneath his dignity. However, Paddy's joy in life is to have a ball or stick thrown for him, and Séamus has managed to bury every ball we buy for Paddy. We have no idea where this burial ground is but by now it must have around three thousand balls in it. I would not be at all surprised one day to see part of the hillside cave in, as an avalanche of balls rolls down on the house.

Séamus is also a shameless thief – he can pick your pocket, and make food left on the table or the kitchen counter disappear. I left the remains of a huge rib roast on the counter while I was saying goodnight to some guests and, when I went back to put it away and clean the pan, I thought at first I was losing my memory and had already done it. The pan was clean.

The roast was obviously in the refrigerator. On further inspection the roast was not in the refrigerator, but there was not a sign of a mess and that pan was sparkling. Séamus was sitting outside the kitchen door, looking totally innocent, but extremely content.

He can do his thieving without leaving a clue. I could not believe how much butter we were using in the kitchen. Then one evening I turned from the stove suddenly and saw Séamus slipping quickly out the door, and I caught a quick glimpse of the butter foil in his mouth. The pound of butter I had opened to cook with was gone, and when I confronted him in the sitting room thirty seconds later there was not a sign of evidence. He had to have swallowed the whole thing foil and all!

Séamus has also very obviously read Lady Susan Hunter-Browne's book, because one cross word and he sulks, well actually he goes into sulks when we have absolutely no idea how we have offended him. When Séamus sulks he does not go off into the garden or fields to do it – he sits in the corner of the room where he can be seen, looking hurt and despondent and refuses for hours to be humoured. This mood can be triggered by anything. If we don't answer the back door quickly enough when he knocks, if we go to town and leave him behind, if we don't have the right programme on television, if we don't take him for a walk at the right time, if we don't have his towel warm enough when he comes in on a rainy day. You name it and Séamus can sulk about it.

And here I am a grown adult, grovelling to humour him and he treats me with scorn until he is ready to forgive me. Actually scorn is not really the word – he looks at me as if I have truly broken his heart and he wants nothing further to do with me, and it is such a relief when he decides to forgive. I always know when the crisis is past. He will come and stand in front of me with his head down, waiting to be petted. Then I pet him and say "Kissee, Kissee", and he stands up with his paws on my shoulder and licks my face, and all is well with the world.

Oh God, I don't believe this, but it's true. I just hope my sons don't find out about this, or they will seriously consider a competency hearing. As I said earlier, "Never get a free dog from a used car salesman, particularly one you have conned, as paybacks can really be hell."

Was it all worth it for three hundred pounds? Well, when I think of the junk heaps I've been stuck with?

And Mopsie makes three.

One summer's day when Paddy and Séamus were about one and a half years old, I saw them playing with a strange looking grey thing out in the back garden. I thought it was some little wild animal and went outside to check. As I walked towards them this little multi-coloured grey creature ran over to me and started wagging its tail. Its fur was matted with cockle burrs and there was a strong odour of cow manure which wafted towards me with every wiggle of its body and wag of its tail. As I looked closer, I could see two bright little eyes shining at me from under some shaggy fur. I had just met Mopsie and I was not impressed.

Over the next few days this strange little creature would show up out of the blue, smelling as badly as ever, play for a while with Paddy and Séamus, and then disappear again. Then one day he didn't leave so I asked Allan to barricade the wrought-iron gate so that he couldn't get into the back garden with the dogs and maybe would get bored and go home. The first barricade didn't work because it wasn't high enough. The little creature just jumped over it. Neither was the second. Allan suggested that the animal might be here to stay, and I replied that if he was around much longer I was going to have to give him a bath in our tub. Horrified at the very thought, Allan went out and built the barricade even higher, and when that didn't work he told me to give the damn dog a bath, he was putting up the white flag in total defeat.

After three changes of soapy water and equal rinsings which put our whole plumbing system in danger of severe blockage, we had a chance to see what this thing looked like. Allan cut the fur from around its eyes and I brushed his coat, and there before us was the cutest little dog with wagging tail and shiny eyes who immediately got named Mopsie by Allan because he said he looked like a dust mop. Over the next week Mopsie was there all the time. He played with Paddy and Séamus all day, but I would not let him in the house at night because I felt it would be wrong in case he wanted to go home. He went out of his way to make up to me, but I was afraid to get too fond of him. I knew he belonged to somebody else, and that it would just be a matter of time before we found his owner.

Then one day the phone rang and this male voice said, "I understand you have my dog."

I said, "Oh, you mean Mopsie."

The male voice said, coldly, "My dog's name is Zuppie!"

He came around to get his dog that afternoon, and the next morning Mopsie was on the doorstep covered in cockle burrs, smelling of cow manure, wagging his tail, and his bright eyes shining! Mopsie's home was about two miles away, through fields with long grass and lots of cows. He looked just as wretched as the first day he arrived.

We fed him, let him play with Paddy and Séamus for a while, gave him a bath, combed his hair and sadly called his owner, who promptly came and got him. We didn't see Mopsie for over two weeks, and every day we expected to see him come bouncing down the driveway or over the garden wall with his tail wagging, his bright eyes shining, and his fur covered in cow shit and cockle burrs.

But it didn't happen. One afternoon I was finishing my correspondence. I had a postcard left that I had picked out to send to a friend in the States which implied that it was her turn to write as I had not heard from her lately. On impulse I addressed it instead to Mopsie and signed it from Paddy and Séamus – I thought it would be funny. I posted it the next day.

The very next evening, just as it was getting dark, I was sitting in the dining room talking to some guests and out of the corner of my eye I caught sight of a little black shape heading down the garden path to the door. This little dark shape was instantly recognisable by the strong odour which preceded him. Mopsie had come back!

The following morning my telephone rang early and sure enough, it was Dick, Mopsie's owner. He wanted to know what time Mopsie had arrived the evening before and, when I told him it had been just about dark, he told me what had happened. He had been sitting by the fire with Mopsie at his feet when he mentioned to Mopsie that he had had some mail that day from Paddy and Séamus. Dick said that as soon as he said "Paddy and Séamus" Mopsie perked up his ears. He was so amused by this that he said "Paddy and Séamus" again and showed Mopsie the postcard. Mopsie immediately went and sat by the door and the next time Dick went to get a bucket of coal, Mopsie was gone.

Dick also went on to say that he wasn't going to bother coming to get Mopsie this time, that we might as well keep the dog, as obviously it didn't love him any more. He sounded so sad that I kept him on the phone and discussed an agreement whereby we both realised that Mopsie was totally independent and was going to do his own thing regardless, and that he would have two homes, coming and going as he chose, and that's exactly what happened.

Mopsie would disappear for hours at a time to visit Dick. He would show up at Barrow House in his own good time. It didn't take him long to start using the road instead of the fields, because he quickly realised that smelling of cow manure meant a bath, and a brushing, which he really didn't care for. The pay-off for him was that once he became socially acceptable I let him sleep in the house. It's not that I'm soft in the head, or anything, but my original sheepskin rug was getting a little crowded and tattered looking because of Paddy and Séamus. So I had to replace it and while I was at it I just thought, to hell with it, and bought three.

Allan and I would spot Mopsie trotting along the side of the road as we were coming to and from Ardfert village. Then one morning I was driving back from the village and there was Mopsie, sitting at the cross-roads, not far from his original home. I swear he was waiting for me so he could thumb a lift! I stopped the car, opened the door, and Mopsie jumped right in on my lap with his paws on the steering wheel, ready to go.

This became a habit of his. Allan and I regularly came back from Ardfert with Mopsie pretending he was driving the car. He still does this, but only rarely, as Dick has since moved and Mopsie doesn't have much reason to wander off. He does however disappear for a while when we are travelling in the winter time. While Dick was still living close by, our caretaker would tell us that he always knew when we were coming home because Mopsie would suddenly show up, and be sitting on the front steps thirty minutes before we came down the driveway, looking as though he was the official reception committee!

Don't ask me to explain this, but Mopsie always knows when Allan is coming back from town. At least ten minutes before Allan's car turns the corner at the end of the bay, Mopsie lets out a bark and heads for the front courtyard wagging his tail. Paddy and Séamus follow. They know that Mopsie is always right, and he is.

Without question the three dogs have taken over our lives. Paddy is "our first born" and he divides his affection and attention equally between myself and Allan, and anyone else who will throw a ball or stone or piece of wood for him. However he would leave us all in a second for a little kid. He simply loves children, and when we have a small guest staying, he shadows them all day and then follows them to the door of the big house when it's time for them to go to bed. He would wait there happily until morning if we didn't make him come inside.

Séamus and Mopsie are different, and much more possessive with their affection. While they obviously love us both, basically Séamus is my dog and Mopsie is wholeheartedly, totally dedicated to Allan.

I have already told you that Séamus is very sensitive and he definitely wants his share of attention from the guests. He is totally disdainful of Paddy's grovelling to get someone to throw a ball and would never stoop to such behaviour. But Séamus gets his attention in a less obvious but more startlingly eye-catching manner – he fishes. Yes, I mean literally fishes in the bay, where everyone can see him perform. He will stand for hours when the tide is low playing with his friends, the crabs and eels and, when he sees a fish, he will go "on point." No he doesn't catch anything, as they are his friends, and I think he would have a complete nervous collapse if he even saw a fish hauled in on a line. The bay is his own little play world and his way of competing with Paddy for the guests' attention.

And Mopsie – well, he will accept attention if it's coming, but there is only one master in his life and that is Allan. Allan takes precedence over absolutely everything, including food. That little dog worships every step his master takes and of course his master, being totally flattered, caters to his worshipping follower. Mopsie has his own chair in Allan's office so he can sit there while Allan reads the *Financial Times* and does his assorted paperwork. When the dogs are fed Allan will stand guard to ensure that Mopsie's bowl is not emptied by two large predatory black Labradors.

Actually Mopsie would be a lot better off if he

missed a meal or two as he is now so chunky that it takes him three tries to jump up on the bed in the morning.

So we now have three "free" dogs . . . ha! There is no such thing as a free dog, there's the vet and the dog licence and the food and the dog sitter when we are gone. The food bill alone makes Allan a valued customer at Quinnsworth grocery store. Breakfast is Pedigree Chum – special cuts of course – but dinner is a much more elaborate affair. Séamus developed what was, for him, a rather embarrassing delicate colon condition which he is very sensitive about anyone even discussing. His vet recommended brown bread in his diet and the only way to make brown bread gastronomically appealing to Séamus was to smother it with meat and gravy. Yes, this means a regular cooked meal for the three of them every evening as we can hardly serve Séamus something more special than the other two. Fortunately they are not too fussy about the meat dish – liver, mincemeat, beef hearts, kidneys, a little chicken and stewing beef now and again, with tuna and noodles on Sunday as a special treat, and they are quite happy! When we leave in the winter I have to cook up large amounts to put in the freezer so our little darlings will still be able to maintain their culinary standards and Séamus will not have a relapse of his "delicate" condition. Between you and me, I think Séamus tricked the vet and it's all a scam but I have noticed that a slice of brown bread a day does wonders for me, so it's easier to go along with the whole thing and not risk a relapse for Séamus.

Yes, there we were retired with everything planned. Summers in Ireland. Winters in the USA or travelling the world. Our children grown up, a little money in the bank, free at last, no commitments and we blew it all with three "free" Irish dogs!

CHAPTER FIFTEEN

THE GARDENERS

I have never worked with my hands and have always had tremendous admiration and awe for people who can. Everyone has some secret dream. Mine grew steadily over the years. I wanted to be a brilliant gardener. Now I realise that the gap between dreams and reality is called effort and commitment regardless of whatever excuses we may make.

Here I was at Barrow House, retired from an office and desk, embarking on a tremendous adventure with Ina, a farmer's daughter, to help me and two books on flower gardens. And, best of all, a gardener/handyman to do the basic work. How could I possibly fail to have grounds to compete with Muckross House or even Kew gardens. It was easy. I brought home some cabbage plants and Ina said, "What are they?" My gardener, as it turned out, didn't know a pansy from a petunia but was strong on vegetables. When I told him where I wanted the cabbages planted, he told me immediately that they would not grow there and I immediately determined that they would – after all I did, at least, know a pansy from a petunia. He was so annoyed by my insistence that the cabbages were to be planted in that particular spot, he went and gathered up the workmen who were still on the grounds, so that they could all convince me of the error of my ways. Not a hope, the more support he gathered up, the more determined I was about the location of the cabbages and that's where they were planted.

The cabbages became a point of pride. I was going to make them grow regardless. Fortunately, they were located by the first part of the pathway, between my boathouse and the main house, so I could keep an eye on them every day and even talk to them as I was passing.

Ina's only involvement with the land, so it seems, had been swiping her father's potatoes. Whenever she needed a few shillings she would go out to one of the fields, dig up some potatoes to sell to her "fence" which was a small store in town, and cover her tracks by sticking the potato plant back down in the ground. What she didn't realise was that some of her brothers and sisters were doing the same thing. One day her father was out proudly walking his fields when he happened on one where, as far as the eye could see, the potato plants were dead as tumbleweed blowing in the desert. He quickly determined that this was not a serious return of the potato blight and the culprits were rapidly identified and punished.

If Ina was good at digging potatoes in her youthful days, she was even better at driving a tractor. If she needed to get to town for the evening and didn't have a ride, she would go to a neighbouring farm and tell them her father needed to borrow their tractor – she would then drive it to the dance and return it the next morning. Fortunately, her father was a very popular man as again there were other talented brothers and sisters. There must have been many a night that every tractor in the area had been loaned to help him out when, in actual fact, they were seen lined up outside the dance hall in town.

Ina and I may have been lacking in gardening skill but we more than made up for it in initiative and enthusiasm. Our pansies were thriving and on the strength of that, we made another swoop to Liscahane garden nursery and bought tray after tray of bedding plants. It didn't matter what they were – if they were flowers, we bought them. We even planted them ourselves as we wanted every bit of the pleasure.

I had an Irish country garden flower book which I had drooled over every night for the past year. We did what it said and put the tall plants either against the walls or in the centre of the flower beds. Other than that we hadn't a clue but we were having a wonderful time being close to nature and the soil.

Then we went for the big time and decided we wanted a rose garden. Not just a few rose bushes but dozens and dozens. By this time, we were well known at the garden centre and it was with restrained amusement that they helped us load the back seat and trunk of my car with every colour and type of rose bush imaginable. When we got home and looked at the enormity of the task of planting our purchase, we decided that maybe we should just mark the place where we wanted them planted and let the gardener take over.

Actually, we let him do it as we were beginning to get a little tired of being next to nature and the soil. This planting frenzy had occurred within the space of a few weeks and watering our new responsibilities was becoming more and more of a chore. Then the drought set in and summer of 1989 was to be the hottest, driest summer in Irish history. When we first planted everything we knew we would have to water for a few days, but then we thought the plants would be on their own. But it didn't happen that way. Dear God, who ever heard of drought in Ireland? Day after day we carried buckets, stretched hoses and looked at the sky, praying for rain. We had planted our flowers with absolutely no skill but with lots of love – they were our babies and we had to protect them and nurture them. I had brought some water hoses from Florida but not nearly enough for the area needed. The Irish hoses I bought in town would not attach to any of the fittings I had, so each day we laboured with buckets in the hot sun, hoping that the next day the clouds would burst.

As week after week passed, with not a drop of moisture from the heavens, it didn't cross our minds to give up as our toils were being rewarded. We had flowers – beautiful, gorgeous, lovely living things that we had watched grow each day and which had only survived because of our back-breaking work. Actually if we had known at the beginning of the drought how long it was going to last, we would probably have just shrugged our shoulders and said, "Well, win some – lose some" and those little hummers would have been left to shrivel in the ground!

But it didn't happen that way and before we realized that we were in over our heads, it was too late because we were committed to our beautiful flowers, not to mention my cabbages which were also thriving much to the disgust of my gardener. He had said they would never grow because they were in the shade – hah! that's what saved them. That and the fact that I stopped and spoke to them every morning and evening as I made my way along the path to and from the main house. That and the fact that he couldn't sabotage them without getting caught as I had clearly informed him that I was watching them closely for any signs of death from unnatural causes.

The only time I ever got the best of Ina was over the watering of the flowers. If I was too tired in the evening to carry buckets of water, I quickly found that all I had to say the next morning to Ina was, "Oh my gosh, Ina, I just came past the pansies and they were crying out for you to give them a drink – they were going "ahhh" and saying they were parched with the thirst." And darn if she didn't run out and water them while I sat in the shade and read the morning newspaper.

There is no question about the fact that Ina and I are "marshmallows." We once spent hours picking periwinkles on the strand and then left them in a bucket by the back door to cook later. When we went to get them for the pot, we found that the little devils had crawled up the sides of the bucket and were well on their way to making their break for freedom. When we saw this, neither one of us had the heart to cook the little critters and we put them back over the sea wall into the tide and haven't picked one since.

This confession of soft-headedness gets worse. I was making out the grocery list one morning and put cabbages at the top. When Ina saw me do that she asked? "What are you buying cabbage for when you have beautiful cabbages fully grown out in the garden?" I froze in horror as the grim words she had spoken sank in. I had personally watered those cabbages every day – I had spoken to them morning and evening as I passed. I had told them what beautiful cabbages they were and how much pleasure they gave me as I watched them grow big and strong and lovely shades of green. In all that time, I had never thought of *eating* them. I tried to tell myself not to be silly and actually went up to my cabbage bed with a knife to cut two heads. But when I got there I simply could not do the deed. I even hid the knife behind my back lest they realised my murderous intent.

When I returned to the kitchen, cabbageless, Ina took the knife from me and said she would take care of the situation. But she was back in the kitchen five minutes later without a cabbage. She couldn't do the deed anymore than I could. It's one thing to eat a cabbage bought in a grocery store, it's another to kill one you know personally.

The gardener, who was having his coffee, listened to us discussing our dilemma and the next thing we knew he had gone and cut two cabbages and there they were sitting on the kitchen counter looking at us.

How he could have done such a thing I have no idea as he was always a sweet, kind, gentle person, except that he had always hated my cabbages!

Yes, I cooked bacon and cabbage for the guests that evening but I didn't eat a bite. I cooked my poor cabbages simply so that they would not have died in vain. But when everyone said how delicious the meal was, I felt terrible pangs of guilt and the worst was yet to come. When dinner was over and the dishes all done I kept putting off the inevitable – the awful walk to the boathouse past the surviving cabbages who by now would be well aware of my treachery.

I didn't turn on the floodlights for the path, hoping that darkness could hide my guilt. But I was out of luck, it was a beautiful moonlit night. There they were standing in their rows, all fat and chunky green with two vacant spaces silently screaming betrayal for all the world to hear. I wanted to speak to them but I couldn't because I knew they had grown big and strong just for me, because they thought I loved them. Now they were standing there with hurt, quiet dignity waiting to see which of them would be next! That night, when I said my prayers, I caught myself just in time. I mean after all how could I expect God ever to take me seriously again if I asked His forgiveness for killing a cabbage!

The next morning I went the long way around to the main house. Once there, I turned from a soppy marshmallow into Attilla the Hun. The rest of the cabbages had to go — it was necessity, it was self-defence. I simply could not face them again, nor could I spend the rest of the summer avoiding them. I asked my gardener to cut the lot right then and take them home to his neighbours. I hate to attribute an evil trait to anyone but I swear I saw a gleam of pleasure in his eye as he took out a large knife from the kitchen to go after my cabbages. When his car went up the driveway, I knew the evil deed was over and done with and I swore I would never get emotionally involved with a cabbage again. And I haven't!

Except for the cabbages and the drought our first venture into gardening was a success. Everyone commented on how beautiful the flowers were and yes they were, but then so were the cabbages. However, I'm not going to mention them again. But before we knew it the summer was gone. The leaves started to change color and fall to the ground and our lovely flowers faded and withered.

As the crows circled and swarmed in bursts overhead we knew our first season was over. With more than a touch of melancholia, Ina and I sat down by the fire in the diningroom and opened a large bottle of wine to soften our sadness. At first we sat in silence and then slowly we started to remember episodes where we had either laughed or been frozen in terror. Before we knew it, we were laughing uproariously with the pure joy and abandon which only true friendship, freedom and good wine can produce. And in the folly of our merriment we planned so many things for the next season. We were going to grow all our flowers from seed and have a real vegetable garden. No, not cabbages, but lots of brussels sprouts, potatoes, tomatoes, lettuce and any other edible thing that we could find in a seed package. We even decided to have chickens and ducks. It wasn't long before turkeys and geese were thrown in also, but a cow was ruled out as neither of us wanted to get up early to milk the darn thing!

After a long winter, which Allan and I spent on a trip around the world as a retirement present to ourselves, it was finally spring again at Barrow. Did the time interval dampen our plans? Not a bit! As a matter of fact time had made our plans more grandiose. We were going to bake apple tarts, make blackberry jam and bottle all our vegetables which would stand neatly in rows on shelves all properly labelled and dated.

We started out that second spring with a new gardener. The previous one had been wonderful apart from his intense dislike of my cabbages. But he had only been working for me part-time while he was waiting for a full-time job in construction and the job he wanted had turned up. I would have written more about him but I am constrained by the distinct possibility that he did not declare his income. Actually, now that I can remember everything clearly, he emigrated somewhere, no one has a forwarding address and his name is lost in the depths of time.

Mike, the new gardener, was employed full-time in his regular job and worked on the side for extra income. Mike was a psychiatric nurse!

It wasn't long before Ina and I realized that we were being thoughtfully analysed on a daily basis and I certainly didn't tell him about my cabbage experience of the previous year. I must admit that my opinion of people who work in mental institutions was strongly influenced by previous professional association. As a student nurse who did an obligatory three month psychiatric affiliation, it didn't take me long to come to the conclusion that a large number of the employees were crazier that the patients could ever hope to be. This opinion was greatly reinforced years later when, as part of my hospital responsibilities, I had a large psychiatric annex to administrate. I had not started out with this assignment but there were four other assistant administrators, all males, and I was late for a meeting one day and drew the short straw.

I went to my first meeting with my new management team in that area, none of whom I had previously met. Not being familiar with the building I thought I had followed directions accurately but when I opened the door to what I had assumed was the conference room I started to withdraw rapidly. It appeared to be occupied by a group of psychotic patients in a catatonic state. Dear Lord, I was in the right room and this was part of my new management staff!

When everyone was assembled the meeting began. Now most of the business in American hospitals which affects clinical areas or policy is first addressed through appropriate committees. These committees are usually very effective, there is always a specific agenda and the usual time frame is one hour. It is also the chairman's responsibility, as with any committee, to ensure the meeting remains focused and on schedule and to reschedule a further meeting if necessary.

I was sitting in on this weekly management session to introduce myself to staff and familiarise myself with the personnel. By the end of the meeting, some three hours later, I was the one who was catatonic! They had spent the whole time discussing who should administer the fund for the weekly movie reward for the children in the adolescent unit. Three hours with no decision made over a fund of approximately *twelve to eighteen dollars a week!* But worse, the discussion was based on *feelings*. Everyone present had their opportunity to express their *feelings* about who they *felt* should be responsible for the safety of this great wealth. Worse still (if it could get worse and it did) everyone also had the chance to express their *feelings* about what everyone else had expressed and how it had affected *their feelings*. This was not a management committee – it was blooming group therapy! Unfortunately I was finally called on to express my *feelings* and my *feelings* were not nice.

If I remember correctly, I believe I told them that in the previous three hours I felt, that as a management group, they hadn't demonstrated enough skill to be able to manage their own bowel movements, let alone manage and be responsible for a large number of employees and patients who were dependant on them for leadership and direction in patient care! As you can no doubt guess, I immediately evoked all kinds of *feelings* but at least they were focused on something more important than *eighteen dollars*!

Actually my first meeting with the group was really a success. Later that day I heard through the grapevine that after I'd left, they had made their first major decision, and in record time. They had decided to put arsenic in my coffee at the next meeting!

Ah well, it was lovely to be retired from all that but how I ended up with a psychiatric nurse as a gardener/handyman was a secret that only God could answer. Not only was Mike a psychiatric nurse but he was also colour blind. When we left for the winter, I left instructions for my boathouse apartment to be re-painted one shade darker peach than what was already on the walls. Fortunately it was dark the evening we returned to Ireland or we would have had to wear sunglasses to dull the glare of the most horrible psychedelic pink.

That was the bad news – the good news was that part of the roof of the boat house had blown off in a storm and the whole thing was covered by insurance and the interior was going to have to be re-painted anyway. I was so happy to be back that I sort of took the whole thing in my stride. I tried not to notice that the bill for painting indicated that it had taken two full weeks to slosh the awful stuff on the walls in the first place.

But it was spring in Ireland and too many exciting things were going on to worry about such little things as a huge hole in the ceiling of the sitting-room and a God awful colour on the walls – it was time for our seed boxes!

Ina and I had bought packages and packages of seeds and we spent days making up the trays and figuring out the best place in the big house to put them so they would sprout up big and strong. Actually we would have been better off spending a little more time reading the directions but who really takes time for that – certainly not us.

While we were making up the seed boxes I noticed a certain rivalry developing between myself and Ina. She had her favourite flowers and it became obvious that she was picking out the best trays and location for her chosen ones. The rivalry got worse each day as we both raced over to the basement of the big house to see whose seedlings were starting to show and whose little green sprouts were looking the healthiest. I swear that if she got there before I did she switched the boxes around and of course I would never have thought of doing that to her!

The seedlings were starting to cause a serious breakdown in our relationship. My nasturtiums would have done much better if they had had the spot on the window ledge and it was her own fault if her delphiniums had got leggy because they had had too much light.

We were trying to keep an air of good-natured banter when in fact we were coming closer and closer to all-out war. And there was Mike the psychiatric nurse, cum-gardener, cum-handyman taking it all in with a bemused smile on his face.

We tried not to discuss anything to do with the current status of our seedlings around him but on his coffee break he would stand leaning against the door with cup in one hand, three cookies in the other and, between mouthfuls and sips, innocently ask if we really felt any of those seedlings were going to make it. It may well have been his routine enquiries about our "feelings" which averted an all-out war between myself and Ina. In Mike we had found a common adversary. Ina's back went up at the implication that her seedlings were less than perfect. My hackles rose when he said "feel" when "think" would have been more appropriate.

After a few weeks of this Ina asked me confidentially if I had noticed that Mike seemed to be constantly mentally assessing us and I replied,

"Of course he is, it's what he is trained to do. He's a bright, young man with lots of textbook knowledge and theory and he's supposed to be using it. He can't just switch on and switch off for the hospital patients – he is in a profession where people are his focus." I asked her if that made her uncomfortable and she said, "Well, I do get the feeling that he thinks we're a little whacko."

My first response was that I certainly hoped so. But when I asked her why she thought this she explained that he had started bereavement counselling about her seedlings and had asked her how she was going to accept the fact that they just weren't going to make it.

Well that did it – Mike was off for four days and we made our first big swoop of the season back to Liscahane Garden Centre. Four days later, when Mike returned, all the flower beds were neatly planted with the healthiest looking little plants which had had the most miraculous spurt of growth in the previous few days. All the seedlings from the basement were gone. Only the empty trays by the flower beds were casually scattered to indicate where they might be relocated. Mike didn't say a word but couldn't hide his puzzlement.

Well, the next planting on the agenda was the vegetable garden where the seeds were to go directly into the ground. Mike prepared the spot for us and came to watch us as we prepared to set the seed. Just as I opened the first packet of carrot seeds he asked, "Why do you feel you want to grow your own vegetables – you can get them in the market much cheaper."

I just snarled and said, "Dammit, because I want to see them grow".

As soon as I said that I felt badly. His smile disappeared and he looked crestfallen, but I made it up to him later that day with the potatoes. I had bought the seed potatoes a week previously and had put them in a dark cupboard just as I had seen my grandmother do. Then I brought them out and cut them in sections, making sure that each one had a good eye in it, and put them in water to soak.

Now Ina had not said a word as she watched me do this but Mike could restrain himself no longer.

"Why did you cut the seed potatoes in sections?" Well, the answer was obviously not because I had made my money from a large potato farm in Idaho but simply because the only one and other time I had planted potatoes was when I had been five years old and that's how my grandmother had done it.

When I explained this to Mike he gave his faintly amused smile and asked me how I planned on planting them. He actually asked me to draw a diagram for him which I did with rising temper. He looked at my drawing of a wedge of earth and listened to my explanation of how I was going to make a hole at the top using a stick and drop a piece of potato in it and cover it over and he just smiled and said, "Well I guess it might work."

We adjourned to the cleared space by the old apple tree in the orchard and, while Mike watched, Ina and I planted our potato crop. When we had finished and Mike was clearing up everything, he asked me, "Why did you *feel* you have to plant potatoes?" I wanted to make a smart remark like, "Because I damn well wanted to." And then I remembered how short I had been with him earlier in the day over the carrots before we had even got to the lettuce, cucumber and runner beans. I remembered all the psychiatric employees I had ever dealt with and what had made them happy and I said, "Because I *feel* I wanted to do it, because I wanted to *feel* the pleasure of the memory. Because I want to *feel* the pleasure of watching something grow. Because I want to *feel* the anticipation and excitement of sticking a fork in the ground and finding a treasure trove of new potatoes hiding in the earth. I wanted to *feel* the joy of having something grow because I put it there." As I paused to watch his reaction, I felt the dirt on my hands and smelt the spring fragrances of a gentle evening breeze in Ireland. and I added, "I've spent the most part of my life having to take responsibility and having to make sound decisions by my head and having to worry whether or not those decisions were appropriate, fair and productive and sometimes in doing so, I had to tear out my heart. But all I'm doing now is planting some potatoes which is truly giving pleasure for my heart. This decision is not going to harm anyone and I don't have to worry about its consequences. Mike, I am playing in the meadow and I intend to play in the meadow any chance I get for the rest of my life."

Mike had been listening to me intently and when I finished, his whole face broke into a beautiful smile. I had made a happy man of him with my *"feelings"* and, you know something, I had told him the truth and I felt good also.

Ina, however, wasn't impressed. Later, when Mike had left, she said "Are you sure you remember that's how your grandmother planted the potatoes, because for the life of me, I've never seen them cut up like that for planting." I assured her that I remembered it exactly because hadn't I been the one who used to cut them up? Now when Ina gets a question in her mind she doesn't give in easily and her parting comment was, "Yes, but do you ever remember getting anything back? Or did you and your grandmother eat lots of soda bread?"

So much for my sceptics' comments because months later she burst into the kitchen one afternoon with a handful of tiny new potatoes exclaiming joyfully, "They're ours, look, they grew!"

She had cheated and had dug up the first potatoes when she knew we were supposed to have done it together as they were my darn potatoes. But we boiled them, laced them with butter and salt and declared them to be the best potatoes ever to come out of Irish soil.

And what had happened to the carrots, lettuce, cucumber and brussels sprouts? Well they had all disappeared long before they could grow to production level. Evidently every bug in Ireland is specialised and each vegetable needs a special spray. While I was trying to figure out which spray should go with which vegetable, my beautiful crop disappeared almost overnight. But it didn't matter as my heart had been in the potatoes all along.

And what happened to the chickens and ducks, the apple tarts and blackberry jam? Well, we do have a lot of wonderful bakeries in town along with excellent butcher shops. Oh, we made a few apple crumbles, even a loaf or two of soda bread, but to put it kindly we found that was not where our talent lay. And as for our chickens and ducks, when we thought it over, we realised they would just be a nuisance and would have ended up being lifetime pensioners with burial rights. We would have named them all and been committed to supporting their progeny for ever.

But potatoes – that's a whole different matter. All you do is cut them in sections with an eye in each one.

Make a hole in the dirt with a stick and wait until they come back to you in glorious mounds of treasure trove. Then laced with salt and pepper and mountains of butter. Why, eating them is close to heaven on earth and even more joyful when you know you've grown them yourself.

CHAPTER SIXTEEN

POACHED EGGS AND
CONTINENTAL BREAKFASTS

The first year and a half, breakfast was not a problem. Well it was, but I didn't know about it. Ina had a wonderful arrangement with the gardener: if she was late he cooked the breakfast. I had no idea this was happening as I never showed up in the kitchen before 10 am. The exception to this was if Ina buzzed the intercom to tell me that we were out of bread or milk or whatever. When that happened, I would plunder my own kitchen supplies and run over in my robe to the big house and throw the stuff in the kitchen window, then go back to bed.

The first season it was very difficult to remember all the supplies a guesthouse kitchen needed. The dining-room was in the basement of the big house and the kitchen was the size of a very small galley, which meant no storage space. I had to shop every day and between breakfast and dinner supplies, it was a nightmare trying to remember everything. Every day the shopping list would start with "toms, pots, bread, milk" and invariably something like tea bags or coffee or juice would get left off. Yet it would seem to me that I was buying up the grocery store and there was never enough room to put everything away. Space was the problem as the kitchen was so crammed that we never could see what we did or didn't have.

We managed and, even though there were a number of close calls, Ina never once had to explain that there were no eggs for breakfast as the fox had eaten our chickens during the night, although she was fully prepared to do so if necessary, as well as explaining that we never served white bread at Barrow House as it was bad for the teeth. Or that she couldn't serve bacon or sausage that day because it was her special saint's feast day, and it was an old tradition in this part of Ireland never to serve meat on that particular day. Yes, Ina's talent and charm were always there as "plan B" in case of impending disaster.

The second season the dining room was moved to its present location in the downstairs of the boat house, directly below what were then myself and Allan's quarters. With the kitchen directly under my bedroom I could hear what was going on. I no longer had a full-time gardener and handyman for Ina to commandeer as a stand in so breakfast became a problem. Also our guest volume was increasing and there were more and more requests for early breakfast.

When I knew an early breakfast had been requested, I would automatically wake up early, look at the clock, and if I didn't hear any noise downstairs, I would start to get anxious. Some mornings I would go downstairs in my night-shirt and get everything started before Ina got there. Then I would disappear before the guests arrived. There were a few times when the inevitable happened and I would be trapped in the kitchen with guests banging on the locked dining room door, and no Ina in sight. I would go tearing out the back door, up the rock garden steps to my place, throw on some clothes, tear back downstairs, calmly unlock the dining room door and say something to the effect of, "Goodness me, I thought I heard someone out here." All the time mentally vowing to physically damage Ina when next I saw her. I never did. As I've already told you, Ina can charm her way out of any predicament.

When Ina left to make more money on the oil rigs, the only replacement I could find could not come early in the morning because of small children, so breakfast was mine, and dinner too!

Now I love to cook, but not breakfast. Breakfast is boring, breakfast is greasy and spitting hot fat ruins clothes. It is the hardest meal to cook and serve to large groups. It requires the use of more plates, cups, saucers, dishes, cutlery, pots and pans than a regular evening meal and the hellish thing is that seventy percent of the guests won't eat it after it's served, although most people say they want it in the first place.

I don't know how many times I have got up early

to cook a full Irish breakfast for a group of golfers who had stayed late in the pub only to have them straggle into the dining room at 7.30 am, wait for their breakfast to be served, then push their breakfast plate aside and just have tea and toast and cereal. Now with due respects to the pig farmers of Ireland, the only people who like an Irish breakfast are the Irish and the English. Americans and Continentals won't eat Irish sausage more than once, and Americans and Australians, for the most part, view the fried tomato on their plate as some suspicious form of deadly fungus! Some guests react to a fried breakfast as loaded with deadly cholesterol and the serving of it to them as a virtual assassination attempt. Most women absolutely refuse to eat a mouthful as well they know that those greasy eggs, bacon and sausages are going to pack themselves right all over the hips, tummy and thighs!

In a nutshell, breakfast was the pits to prepare. There was no reward in the sense of satisfaction for the cook, only stacks of greasy plates and lots of leftovers which even my dogs were sick and tired of; they were refusing to answer any call to the kitchen door prior to 1 pm in the afternoon, when they knew that the kitchen would be nice and clean and the garbage disposed of!

Two months after Ina left, I was in London for a quick trip, and lo and behold, what did I see in my expensive hotel – continental breakfast served buffet style. The buffet was included in the hotel room charge and consisted of cereals, fruit, juice, cheeses, assorted breads and, of course, tea and coffee.

A full breakfast was available at a cost of six pounds fifty pence – and not a soul did I see order one in the three days I was there. So it was back to Barrow, and a change of morning routine. I set up a menu which consisted of the London buffet but I also included cream cheese, smoked salmon, yoghurts and cold cuts of meat. The response was wonderful, the dogs and I were overjoyed, and the guests liked it too! I did not offer a cooked breakfast at additional charge. I would have had to price it somewhere around five thousand dollars, as that is what it would have taken at that point to get me to handle another frying pan!

Marie, who was at Barrow House at the time, said it would never work, and Allan was of a similar opinion, but I grimly insisted it would. Now, remember that the majority of my guests are golfers and on that side of forty where the immortality of youth begins to be in doubt. They are affluent, successful in their careers, athletically inclined, and like to feel and look good. They were absolute naturals for my continental breakfast.

It cost me a fortune, but I didn't mind. As I've said before, one of my mottos is, "Hell, if you can buy your way out of a problem, do it." And I did it. It did not bother me a bit to see mountains of smoked salmon disappearing down French gullets, or whole wedges of cheese and baskets of fruit being discreetly removed for a light lunch or evening cocktail munchies – it was wonderful. My guests were happy and I was ecstatic. No more blooming greasy frying pans for me, and my dogs could once again go for a long walk without being winded!

I crowed about my success every day to Allan and Marie until they finally told me that if I said "continental breakfast" one more time they were both going to leave the country and, worse, Marie was going to leave her six children with me. As a compromise they let me say "CB" but still glowered at me when I said it. Marie wanted to know what she was supposed to do if someone asked her for a cooked breakfast, and I told her to just look horrified and whisper in hushed, shocked tones that "We don't serve 'that stuff' here."

"Right" she said and gave me her look.

We told everyone in our literature and on registration about the "CB" but it was bound to happen sooner or later that someone was going to test my strength of will and I'm not sure who was testing me the most. One morning, with a guest behind her, Marie came to the kitchen, where I was enjoying a cup of coffee and a cigarette, and said very sweetly, with a lovely innocent smile, "Oh, Mrs Erde, this lady wants to know if she can have an egg."

"Oh, my goodness," said I with an equally sweet, innocent smile, "we haven't had an egg in the place since that horrible salmonella and staph epidemic which killed all those people in England." After all,

Ina is my cousin, and some of it is in the blood, and the rest has just rubbed off!

Well, everything goes in cycles, or so they say, and my CBs were wonderful for a while, but I found myself adding more and more to the buffet for the very same reason I disliked cooking breakfast. It gets boring to handle the same food every day. I truly like to see my guests enjoy their food. I even bought chafing dishes and set out hot buffet items and, in a few seasons, my "CB" was such an elaborate affair that it was costing me a fortune, and giving me more hassle than fried breakfasts ever did. The waste was beyond belief. I had the most constipated dogs in Kerry because I fed them all the outdated cheese, and if anyone offered them some smoked salmon, even today, I think my dogs would bite them.

So at the beginning of this last season, I switched back to fried breakfasts, and my first guests of the season were repeat French guests. I welcomed them into the dining room for breakfast, and told them their eggs, bacon and sausages would be right out after they had finished their cereal.

And he said "Oh, that would be lovely, but could we please have our smoked salmon first?" I didn't have any damn smoked salmon, but fortunately Allan did, and so I raced over to our kitchen in time to whisk the last of his supply right out from under his nose and open mouth. I guess it's no wonder he calls me and the staff Ali Baba and her forty thieves!

Breakfast is my least favourite meal to prepare, but

eggs scrambled, boiled or fried are duck soup compared to poached eggs. Requests for poached eggs have popped up at the worst possible times. Just thinking about them can give me heartburn. In fact it was poached eggs that finished me with cooked breakfasts in the first place.

I had some guests who stayed several weeks. They were the most delightful people, but they had an awful habit of coming down to breakfast at one minute to 10 am, and always had a different breakfast request. The two of them always wanted eggs but, if one wanted boiled, the other wanted scrambled. They rarely ate bacon, or sausage, but if there was none saved for them they wanted some, and they would rarely leave the dining room before 11.30 am. In short, feeding these two breakfast was a pain in the rear, and incredibly time-consuming. Their schedule and requests meant that the kitchen and dining-room could not be cleaned up and finished with until noon. Half my day was gone on two breakfasts.

The young lady who was helping in the kitchen was terrified of the couple because he was chief executive officer of one of the Fortune 500 companies, and seemed very grumpy when he wasn't at all. His wife was very glamorous and wore designer sports outfits set off to perfection by her fabulous diamonds. Now my young Irish lady was pretty as a picture, smart as a whip, with the most delightful personality but she was completely intimidated by them. I worked for days to build up her self-confidence so that I could delegate these last two breakfasts of the morning to her and I could get on with my other chores and errands in town. Finally, one morning I convinced her that since there was bacon and sausage warm in the oven, she wouldn't have a bit of trouble making a scrambled or fried egg for them. There was nothing to do but to smile, and just cook the damn things the way they wanted them!

I got my shopping list for town and was just turning my car to go out the driveway when I caught a glimpse out of the rear-view mirror of my young lady running towards the car, her arms waving wildly. I stopped the car and this young lady, who I don't think had ever sworn in her life, practically threw herself in the car window screaming, "They want f—king poached eggs." My young lady quit that day! I was able to coax her back but never for breakfast.

That was the first of my many disastrous encounters with poached eggs. In the last year, these encounters are getting more numerous.

My first large group of the past season was made up of fourteen wonderful Australians. Eric Head, from Melbourne, had been a guest with his beautiful wife the year before, and had promptly gone back home to Australia and rounded up all his golfing buddies from Kingston Heath golf club, and convinced them that they had not lived until they had played the Tralee Golf Club and stayed at Barrow House.

Eric put so much time and effort into organising the group that winter that I wanted absolutely everything to be perfect for him and his friends. In the meantime I was spending my winter knee-deep in mud in the middle of the latest renovation project. It was touch and go whether everything would be ready for their May arrival. As a matter of fact, it was a serious nightmare which I never want to live through again. My builder kept telling me "not to worry" but my money was disappearing right, left and centre, and all I could see for it was mud, some concrete, and more mud! The day before the group arrived we were just close enough to completion to fake it. Hell, I had to fake it as there simply was no other choice.

I hired a musician and threw on a big reception for their arrival as, let's face it, warm hospitality covers a multitude of sins. They were an absolutely fabulous group, and enjoyed themselves into the wee hours of the morning. As we cleared up after them I told the staff not to bother coming until 8 am as we surely wouldn't see anyone before 10 am. Wrong.

As I went into the dining room at 7 am, two bright eyed and bushy-tailed Aussies followed me in the door and were shortly joined by six more, all looking for coffee, juice and breakfast.

I scurried around, threw on toast, bacon and pancakes and, to my horror, every fuse in the kitchen kept blowing. It was the first time the kitchen had been used with the new wiring for the additional area. I managed to keep my head, pulled out a chair so I could reach the fuse box, and tried to fix breakfast alternating the use of the stove, coffee pot and toaster, and jumping up to the fuse box whenever I misjudged the circuit load. I finally made it. Sausage, pancakes, toast and coffee were all served before 8 am. Then one late-comer walked in the door, looked at everyone else's plates and said, "Sorry I'm late, but just a poached egg on toast will be fine!"

I must have given him a hell of a look because he changed his mind quickly and settled for pancakes and sausages. My staff arrived promptly at 8 am and I, at 8.01 am, collapsed shaking on my bed, not knowing whether to laugh or cry, but certain that I was going to kill an electrician in the most vicious, cruel possible manner!

But poached eggs had not done with me yet. About two weeks later, two couples arrived at 8 pm. Allan showed them to their suites, and they left right away for dinner at the Tankard. They didn't return until about 11 pm and, as I was still up, I went over to their suites to introduce myself and ask if they had everything they needed.

One couple was absolutely delightful, but when I knocked on the door of the second suite, I could hear this pacing up and down, and then the door was flung open, and a woman was standing there, angry as hell. Nothing, but nothing, was right, including being too close to the ocean, and she had asthma!

I didn't get a chance to say anything, but when she

slammed the door in my face, I had the distinct impression that she was not a happy camper.

The next morning I was a nervous wreck. I am just not used to having guests who are anything but delighted with Barrow House. It has happened from time to time but it is so rare that, when it does happen, it is such a shock it's like having a rattlesnake jump out of the bushes and bite me.

I dreaded her coming over for breakfast but fortunately the nice couple arrived first. They were telling me what a lovely place I had, and how much they were enjoying Ireland when, out of the corner of my eye, I caught sight of their travelling companions heading towards the dining room. She was trucking along with her head down like a bull going into the ring, and he whom I hadn't so far met was following along at the same pace, looking very grim.

I pretended not to see them and went on with the nice conversation I was having with their travelling companions, who were still waxing lyrical about Barrow House. The two charging bulls pulled up short when they came into the dining room and heard the remains of the conversation. I welcomed them to breakfast with a gracious smile, and suggested they help themselves to fruit and cereal while I got fresh coffee from the kitchen for them.

Now I already had everyone in the kitchen on Red Alert. Róisín carried out the coffee to their table with the sweetest smile an Irish colleen in sheer terror can muster. I scrambled the eggs in a jug as I wanted them to be absolutely freshly cooked when they went out onto their table. As I was scrambling the eggs, I happened to look over at my egg trays and made a mental note that I would have to replenish my stock that day. Then I got totally carried away with my role as gracious Innkeeper and decided to kill with kindness. I went out to the dining room to enquire if they wanted sausage and tomato as well as Irish bacon or anything else with their breakfast. The nice couple replied that they only wanted cereal and fruit, and that my homemade muesli was the best they had ever eaten. I don't have homemade muesli – it comes in a package from the grocery store, and the brands get mixed up when the bowl gets low. However, I smiled, graciously accepted this compliment, and turned to the other couple to enquire how they felt about bacon, sausage and tomato.

The grim faced man said, "No thank you, I'll just have two poached eggs." I stood frozen in shock. She then piped up and announced she just wanted one poached egg. In a flash I saw my empty egg trays and the jug filled with freshly scrambled free range eggs just waiting to be cooked in wonderful Irish butter. With complete lack of composure I squeaked in horror "Poached eggs!" They both looked up at me as if I was the dumbest creature God could possibly have made. He evidently assessed the situation, and having decided that I didn't know how to cook a poached egg, said with obvious disgust, "Oh well, never mind, just fry them sunny side up – you do know what sunny side up is, don't you?" He was so pompous, and she was wriggling around in her chair like a little wet hen with a serious itch problem. I knew I couldn't explain that poached eggs and fried eggs were not exactly the problem. The problem was every damn egg I had was already scrambled, and getting them back in their shells would be a little difficult!

I couldn't say a word and barely made it back into the kitchen before I totally cracked up laughing. Róisín and Ramona, already tense from the Red Alert were scared to death when they saw me convulsed with laughter. I couldn't speak. I was laughing so hard the tears were streaming down my face. Every time I tried to explain, I got more hysterical with laughter. The looks on their faces just made me worse. There was no doubt about it, I had lost it. I had lost it, but I still had two guests sitting in the dining-room, expecting their fried eggs to appear before too long. I pulled myself together enough to ask one of the girls to go out the back and get me some eggs from the refrigerator in our apartment. She came back with three which was all there were, and to make matters worse their age was dubious.

How I ever managed to cook those eggs without breaking the yolks, while all the time my tears fell into the pan, I shall never know. By the time I served them I had no make-up left except for mascara streaks across my nose, my eyes were streaming red and my body moved in strange contortions. I simply could not stop laughing.

I realised that I wasn't just laughing about the poached eggs, I was laughing at every bloody miserable thing that had gone wrong since I had become an Irish innkeeper. Oh I had laughed many times before, but this time I had one and a half years of the Kerry County Council "Planning Commission," an architect, a builder, contractors, a winter and spring of non-stop Irish rain, another damn tax audit, no curtains on my windows (because the window company had put the frames in back to front, and they leaked like sieves, and would be fixed whenever). For many, many other things I laughed and the floodgates broke. The tension was gone, and I was ready for another wonderful season.

I did have to explain to the guests what had happened, and fortunately they thought it almost as funny as I did.

And why was my little lady so angry? Well, she had been travelling the world for six weeks with these golf addicts, and she had never played golf in her life. I thought she was an incredibly gracious lady, as every day she had been left to her own devices while the other three stormed yet another golf course. Any non-golfing judge would have let her off with justifiable homicide if she had done the whole lot of them in!

And as to my problem with breakfast, well after trying it all, and doing it my way, I am now going to finally copy the experts – continental breakfast buffet included with suite, and for cooked breakfast – Master Card, Visa, cash or billed to room will be fine.

Breakfast hours: 6.30 – 7.30 Continental
breakfast only
7.30 – 9.30 Continental and
Full breakfast available
poached eggs optional

Breakfast prior to 6.30 am – Dining room doors will be open and guests will be requested not to make a lot of noise as they help themselves to fruit and cereal!

CHAPTER SEVENTEEN

THE TAXMAN COMETH

I opened my mail one beautiful sunny day and found a notice that the VAT man was going to pay me a visit. VAT stands for Value Added Tax which I have to pay to the Irish Government on any revenues produced by my little venture and their representative was obviously going to arrive to check my records.

Now the Internal Revenue in the USA strikes terror in most hearts, mine included, but I really had had only a few dealings with them. (This statement is now out-dated as of September 1995.)

One of the occasions was when I had to get a tax clearance to leave the country for a holiday in the Bahamas. This procedure is no longer required, but it was then. As I was waiting for my turn with the agent, I noticed the gentleman ahead of me. He was having an awful time at the hands of the tax lady. She was about sixty years old, and wore a bright red, crooked wig that matched her lipstick. Her arms and neck were loaded with cheap costume jewellery. This lady definitely was having an identity crisis about her age.

As I watched and listened, I noticed that she smiled continuously while she maliciously goaded this man to lose his temper, and all the time she spoke in the sweetest, softest tone. I started to pray that he wouldn't lose his cool, but he did and stormed out, which was exactly what she wanted, and exactly the wrong thing for him to do.

I was next, so I approached her cautiously, determined to get my business taken care of quickly as I had my tax records in my hands, and what I needed was just a formality. I was leaving the country for two weeks to stay at the Lucayan Bay Hotel in Freeport, Grand Bahama Island. Sound simple? No, she refused to process my clearance because I didn't know the name of the road the hotel was on, and yes I lost my cool!

Another time, out of the blue, the head of the finance department at the hospital where I worked came to my office and told me the IRS had garnished seven hundred dollars of my pay cheque. I thought he was playing a joke at first, as I was a payroll tax deduction employee, and there was no way I could owe the government a penny. In fact I always got refunds as I never claimed myself as a deduction.

Well, without any explanation, they took seven hundred dollars of my money, and when I contacted the local tax office, no one could address my query.

From time to time I received form letters from various people stating that they were referring my question to another office. Then about a year later, again out of the blue, I received a Government refund check for six hundred and eighty eight dollars . . . I never said anything about the missing twelve dollars for fear of further involvement!

Everyone has a certain amount of apprehension when dealing with any Government or similar authority when an inspection is announced. In the twenty years I was involved in hospital administration, we had numerous visits from State licensing authorities and other agencies, but the "biggie" was always the survey by the Joint Commission on Hospital Accreditation.

These people could close your hospital, or get you fired, or just make your life a misery, depending on what they found. I do not know of any hospital administrative staff who did not go into these surveys with symptoms of colitis, loaded with tranquillisers and knees sore from praying. There may have been some out there, but I doubt it. I even know of one director of nurses who carried an Alka Seltzer tablet in her pocket so that if the going got too tough she could just pop it in her mouth, and when it foamed she could fake a seizure. Another that I know of got carted off to the coronary care unit with chest pain in the middle of a survey, and she wasn't faking!

Anyway, all this is to show my reader that I have

been exposed to extreme stress in the past, but the first impression I had of the pending arrival of the VAT man did not strike terror in my heart.

My apprehension began to mount when I started to hear words of consolation at my impending doom. My electrician felt so sorry for me that he forgot to write a bill. Deirdre and Mike at my Ardfert village store couldn't have looked at me more forlornly if they had heard through the grapevine that I was dying of a combination of AIDS, cancer and dengue fever, and my husband had run away with the milkmaid. I started to get distinctly nervous!

Everyone in my little area had heard of my "trouble" and everyone had horror stories about the VAT man. These stories got worse when I was asked the name of my inspector; apparently I had drawn the worst of the lot.

The day finally arrived, and down the driveway came my man. By then I was expecting Attilla the Hun, and had popped a few Verbena Tranquil Life pills from the health food store. I'd also made a sizeable investment in candles at the church but, when he stepped out of his car, I felt a little foolish as here was a very nice looking young man, dressed very smartly. He even looked like my youngest son.

That motherly impression lasted about twenty-six seconds – this nice young man was a trained killer. Hell, he didn't have a mother – he was born in a test tube, and raised in a kennel on raw meat. Worse still, I think the raw meat got withheld for two days before the inspection.

Joint Commission, State Licensing Authority, Internal Revenue. Hah! True terror is the Irish VAT man. They are programmed to resist all kinds of Irish charm, and to sniff out all the imaginative Irish tax avoidance tricks. They would shop their grandmother or parish priest and they start with the premise that everyone is guilty. They are not going to stop until they find out how guilty.

I'd approached this inspection with a basic sense of security. I knew I was totally innocent of deliberate wrongdoing. But I was ignorant about Irish tax procedures. When he sat down to look at my books, apprehension turned to stark terror. My knees shook first, and then my whole body took up the tremors. My heart palpated wildly and it felt like my face was contorted with huge nervous ticks. And I cursed myself for not having an Alka Seltzer handy. It was nine-thirty in the morning but when he settled himself I headed straight for the kitchen, and the vodka bottle, for a quick slug.

The original notice stated that the inspection would last about two hours, but he stayed and stayed and stayed, and I slugged and slugged and slugged.

After what seemed a lifetime, he went as abruptly as he came and I was left legless from a combination of booze, tranquillisers, terror and relief. I used to have an associate in Tennessee who, when she had had a really bad day, would announce at the end of it that she felt as though she had been "Raped by a Baarh". I always laughed when she said this but privately felt it was a little unbecoming for a lady. But hell, Mary Lou, that damn Baarh done and got me too! I know just the feeling. But my Irish bear could whip your bear's ass any day!

In all fairness to the Irish tax man he must have a devil of a job. Everyone in the world hates to pay taxes. But the Irish hate it more than most people. They remember English landlords and evictions. Also Irish taxes are so punitive that for some it is almost justifiable to sneak a few pounds behind the tax man's back.

Now I was in a foreign country, and the last thing I wanted to do was break the law so I started out from scratch with an accountant. I have had many people ask me what was the hardest part of starting up and running an inn in Ireland. Take my word, it's the paperwork, and trying to comply with Irish regulations. After five years of struggle, I am still ignorant and dependant on an accountant and a book-keeper, and have never been able to shrug off the feeling I am not quite legal, and not too far from the slammer. Maybe it's just menopausal neurosis. Or maybe it's because I never felt secure from the very beginning. The first year my accountant did everything for me. I just took the VAT forms and my records in to him, and he was supposed to send them off every two months. Then one day I opened my mail and had a letter that said if I didn't pay up, the bailiff was coming. I drove hysterically into town to tell my accountant my disastrous news, but he was completely unfazed by the whole thing. He simply asked me if it was a red letter or a green letter. I showed it to him, and when he saw it was a green one, he told me not to worry, as it would be months before the bailiffs came, and he would have it all straightened out by then.

There was nothing I could do but leave the matter in his hands, but it did affect my sleep pattern. Then the awful day came when the red letter arrived. By the time I got to his office, I was mumbling incoherently. Again, he told me not to worry, he would take care of it, but my nerves were wrecked. The next morning a car came down the driveway with a man in it, and I told the lady who was working for me that I hoped it wasn't the bailiff. She assured me that when the bailiff came there were usually four men in the car to help carry off the stuff. She was an authority, as that's how her husband's boat went!

Later that afternoon, while my guests were sunning themselves in the courtyard, another car came driving in and out got four men. I knew I was ruined, that I would be the shame of the neighbourhood, and that my guests would tell everyone in America and I'd never have another customer. I ran out to beg for mercy and explain that it was just a mistake, and met the local candidate for the county council, who was out campaigning with three of his supporters! I took all his literature, shook everyone's hand and babbled like an idiot that I would be delighted to vote for him. It wasn't until afterwards when I read the pamphlet that I realised I had just promised to vote for Sinn Féin, the political wing of the IRA! Oh well, it could have happened to anyone, and I can't vote in Ireland anyway.

I now have a bookkeeper who does my VAT returns and keeps my records, and all I do is turn the whole lot over to my accountant at the end of each year. I have no idea what he does with my stuff, but I get a huge bill from him and, after I pay it, I get a tax form that tells me I don't owe anything. Of course the reason I don't owe anything is because I don't make anything. I spend it all on Barrow House. My accountant also gives me an annual lecture on the fact that I am going to go broke!

Now you may wonder why I keep this guy – well, it's simple – I really like him. Ned is the most confirmed pessimist I have ever met in my life. He is the original man who saw a light at the end of the tunnel and recognised it, not as sunshine, but as an express train coming at full speed. This man is a challenge to me, and a tremendous incentive. One day I shall convince him about the benefits of optimism and one day I'm going to make so much money at Barrow House that he will have to eat every word of warning. If I don't manage that I'll have a lot of fun trying!

I'm probably going to have to settle for the "fun trying" as, quite frankly, Barrow House was never intended to make money. It has to pay its own way, but it gives me a lifestyle for six months of the year that is absolutely delightful, and the other six months we go back to the U.S.A. and travel to other places. The fact is, in the winter we go out to the rest of the world, and in the summer, the rest of the world comes to us. Now can anyone, who is not an accountant, think of a better lifestyle? If I had the money in the bank, drawing interest, then I would just have to worry about it without getting any pleasure. And besides, I can't imagine what I would do with my time. As it is, I own the most beautiful piece of property which is appreciating in value, I am developing a business which must add to the value, and I am slowly restoring a lovely old place which owns part of my heart. On top of that, my husband and I are very happy. My accountant says "Bullshit" with his eyes every time I tell him all of the above. He just has no romance or spirit of adventure in his soul.

Well, come to think of it, he must have some. He is handsome as hell, has lovely twinkling eyes and a charming voice, a beautiful wife and four lovely children. I have just realised what is going to happen to Ned. He will hit mid life-crisis, discover the effects of a can of Seven up, sell everything he owns and take

his family and a sailboat around the world, or
something similar. And then he will know exactly why
I do what I do. And it will serve him right and it will
be even better if he has a young accountant who
doesn't understand.

How's that for an Irish curse?

CHAPTER EIGHTEEN

THE PERILS OF AN IRISH TELEPHONE

When I finished the boathouse apartment and stayed there by myself that early fateful week, I knew I needed a telephone so that I could communicate with the outside world. There was already a phone line there and a telephone which was disconnected. I did not think that requesting a phone of my own would be a complicated process. One of the truly wonderful things about Ireland is that you can start out on a simple errand, and end up having the most incredible adventure.

It's a wonderful adventure, if you have a sense of humour. But a nightmare if you don't. Ireland is totally wasted on a humourless person, and they should never set foot in the country except on a tour bus.

In March, 1988, I went to the local telephone office and made my request for a phone. The very pleasant young lady asked me the old telephone number. I had no idea what it was. It seemed important that I produce this information so I volunteered to drive back out to Barrow and look at the phone that was there to see if the number was written on it. It wasn't, so I drove back into town to relay this information. The nice young lady and I then proceeded to search through old telephone books until we found a listing for the previous owner. We looked for some time and finally found a number. Then the nice young lady went to a card index file, and told me that the card was missing. When I asked her what the significance of that was, she told me I couldn't get a telephone until the card was found, because there might be an outstanding bill on it, but I was assured that she would keep looking. I was only going to be in the country one week. Obviously I was going to be without a telephone. No problem, not to worry, I would get one eventually. Eventually was August 1988!

In March of 1989, when I was organising my guest-house for its first season, we had some terrible spring storms which knocked out telephone lines for miles around. I didn't get alarmed the first week my phone was out, as the area had been badly hit. The second week I used a friend's phone to check on the prospects of my line being repaired, and was told that it would probably be the end of the week, if I was going to be at home, so I stayed home. At the beginning of the next week I drove into town to the telephone office. I told this very nice man my problem and how long I had been without a telephone. He then asked me if I would be at home the next day. I started to say "yes" but something stopped me and I said instead "Will it do me any good?" He obviously paused to think, and then his eyes twinkled, and his face broke into a gentle smile. "Not really," he said, "I just wanted to make you feel better. It's been St. Patrick's Day, and Easter, and everyone's taking their holidays. We'll get your line fixed, but I can't promise when."

How could I do anything but smile at this lovely man, and say, "Thank you." I got my phone back in working order the following week.

My next adventure with the telephone company came a few months later. I needed an extension from my boathouse apartment to my office in the basement of the main house. The workmen came out and worked busily until the extension cable reached a point just outside my office window, then everything stopped. I was called aside by the foreman of the crew and told that he had been instructed to go no further. I was to call his supervisor at the telephone number he gave me.

Somewhat surprised, I did as directed and was even more surprised when I was told I couldn't have an extension phone because it was an external extension and they weren't doing those anymore! According to the supervisor, I needed to have a twelve hundred pound piece of equipment installed, so that I would be able to communicate between my office and the boathouse! I pointed out that there was already a piece of cable hanging outside my office window, that if someone would just put a telephone on the end of it, my problems would be solved. But nothing doing. My telephone crew left, leaving the wire hanging outside my office window – the temptation was too much!

Now there is many the home in the USA that has many the extension put in by talented "friends." Here I was in a country where I had a large number of potentially talented friends. Would God have faulted me for doing what needed to be done? Ina could make contact with the needed person, and I didn't have twelve hundred pounds to waste. Twenty-four hours later the contacts arrived. The price to begin with was four hundred pounds but we negotiated down to fifty pounds. I offered to provide the phone from another extension that I did not need. Thirty minutes later I was in business, with a phone in my office and a blood oath sworn that I would go to my grave with my lips sealed as to the name of the person involved. Actually that was no difficult oath to swear. Ever since I took the Dale Carnegie memory course years ago, I have had a hell of a time remembering anyone's name correctly!

The extension worked beautifully the first season. The next year we didn't need it, as we had moved my office over to the boathouse, and the bottom of the boathouse had been converted to a beautiful, more spacious, guest dining-room. I was able to get an extension phone from upstairs to downstairs without any problem. However, after about a month or so, we started getting a lot of crackling and interference on the line. Both Ina and I knew that it had to be from that other line which we were not supposed to have. But how could we call Telecom Eireann about our present trouble without them finding the unauthorised line?

Ina thought for a while and then said, "Not to worry, call and report trouble on the line." So I did and when the telephone van came down the driveway she said to me, "Look mean and hateful when I bring the repairman through the dining-room." So when they came through I glowered but I did notice that Ina was acting very timid and almost subservient as she introduced the repairman. She told me who he was as if I didn't already know he was coming. And as if she was an eighteenth century peasant working in the Big House! The repair man was a nice wholesome looking young Irishman who behaved as if he was trying to look nonchalant around a rattlesnake.

They both disappeared upstairs and about thirty minutes later my young repair man came down through the dining-room, and told me quickly as he was heading for the door that it was all taken care of. I couldn't resist asking him innocently what the trouble had been and he just mumbled quickly as he fled, "Oh, it was just some old wires that needed to be taken down." Well, he had that right!

A few minutes later Ina appeared, not behaving at all like an eighteenth century peasant, and I asked her what the hell was going on. She laughed and said, "Well, we couldn't let him find that extension to the

Big House and have him report it, so I just met him in the courtyard, and told him that while you were gone this winter I was so afraid over in the big house by myself that this friend of mine had arranged to have that extension put in for my safety. And after you got back, I had forgotten to have it taken out and if you ever knew about it you would fire me because you were such a stickler for law and order and doing things properly."

God help us if Ina was Prime Minister of Ireland. The country would rule the world, or the whole country would be in jail as the result of unanimous UN action. With my cousin Ina it would be a toss-up – but the whole world would have a good time either way, and would have no idea of what had happened to it.

However, even though the "old wires" had been removed, I still had trouble with my telephone. It seemed as though every time the wind blew my line went out. I was continually picking up my phone to make sure I still had a dial tone. This may seem slightly paranoid but it is impossible to be in the guesthouse business if people are not able to contact us for reservations.

My fax machine went silent for three weeks which was most unusual. I kept checking the line and looking to see that the electricity supply to the machine had not been turned off. And everything seemed fine – the only problem was that I wasn't getting any faxes. Just as I was about to accept the fact that no one wanted to make reservations, that I was going to go broke, I accidentally found the cause of the problem.

Yes, the phone line was fine and the fax machine had electrical supply. But the two were not connected. Sure enough, when the line from the fax to the telephone outlet was mended with electrical tape, my machine started to work overtime spewing out a gratifying number of reservations requests. I went from penury to possible solvency in the space of a week.

My darling little puppy, Paddy, had chewed through the telephone line from the fax machine. Fortunately for him he had left the line to the electrical socket alone or he would now be just a memory.

This episode naturally made me even more concerned about checking the status of our communication system on a very regular basis. Whenever my phone went out because of a storm or high wind, it usually took at least three days to get it back in working order. The worst part of it was, even though I have two lines, when the phone went out the fax went also.

During my second summer as an Irish innkeeper I found myself almost apologising to the phone company about my problem with my telephone which kept going dead. It was all very mysterious as we were long past the time of year for storms or high winds.

Again, quite by accident, I discovered the cause. There was some construction going on up the hill by the golf club and the heavy equipment going up and down the road was cutting my line, which reached from a telephone pole across the road over my fields and down into the back of the house. When the construction was completed, I heaved a huge sigh of relief. Then I saw a very large, tall hay wagon going down the road and, sure enough, there went my telephone line again. I was extremely upset and relayed my feelings to Telecom Eireann in less than ladylike language. But they forgave me anyway and fixed the line in record time.

The very next morning I had a call from the American Embassy in Dublin making reservations for a Congressman and his wife to stay four nights the following week. I had only been a year and a half in business and I was going to get a congressman as a guest. Hey, that was success. My delight knew no bounds.

For the next few days I had a daily call from the Embassy clarifying details of arrival, payment etc which I tried to handle as though it was a usual occurrence to have celebrities and just something we could take in our stride.

Exactly one day before my congressman was due to arrive, it was announced on the early morning news that the Iraquis had invaded Kuwait. That afternoon I saw a huge hay wagon go down the road, I picked up my telephone and the line was dead! Now what were my chances of an American congressman staying at a place which had no communication with the outside world when his country might be going to war? Absolutely none, zero, zilch.

I looked at that hay wagon, totally overloaded, as it wound down the road. So totally overloaded that it wobbled as it went and my switch flipped. I grabbed my car keys, yelled to my husband that "I'm going to slaughter them" and took off towards my car in the front courtyard. Actually what I had really said was, "I'm going to kill the f . . . king bastards." So I whipped the car around and headed up the driveway in hot pursuit of my telephone wreckers. With blood in my eye and murder in my heart, I caught up with the hay wagon just after it had made the turn for Ardfert.

The hay wagon was slowly ambling along and once I caught up with it I had to slow down. I couldn't pass and cut in front because the wretched thing took up most of the width of the road. As I looked at the back of this hay wagon, the thought crossed my mind (as it surely has for any dog that chased a car), "Now that I've caught it, what the hell am I going to do with it?" Fortunately, it turned in to a farmyard before I ran out of steam. I pulled right in behind it, jumped out of my car, slammed the door hard behind me and marched with determined purpose towards the driver like Wyatt Earp at the OK Corral. Oh, hell, the driver was one of my neighbours who always saluted with a wave and a smile whenever we passed on the road. I couldn't possibly be rude to such a nice man but I had to say something. I said a little feebly, wishing I were somewhere else, "Jimmy, why the hell do you keep loading your hay truck so high that it takes down my telephone line?" I knew him by name because that's who everyone said he was when I described him.

Jimmy looked totally surprised. "I'm sorry," he said "I didn't know that I did."

"Oh, Jimmy, this is the second time in weeks this has happened," I said feebly. I was interrupted by a voice and a face at the top of the haystack. "We didn't take down your line at all. The telephone company are up there working on your line – I saw them myself."

I tried to maintain my dignity while mumbling my apologies but all shreds of it were wiped away when Jimmy said plaintively, "Why do you keep calling me Jimmy when my name's not Jimmy at all?"

I slunk back to my car with my tail between my legs. Damn, the one and only time I had ever gone charging through the neighbourhood fit to kill and I had had to be wrong.

As I drove back to Barrow, I caught a glimpse of myself and the total change in my lifestyle. Here I was, once a Director of nursing and later a hospital administrator in the USA, now living in the Irish countryside chasing hay wagons like a mad dog. But isn't that the joy of it all? Isn't life wonderful? And yes, my telephone line was out because Telecom Eireann was simply moving the telephone pole so that I would have no further problems. That darn pole had been in that one place for umpty-nine years and they had had to pick that day to move it.

Oh well, I've had no further troubles with my line and to this day, I don't know what Jimmy's name is. As soon as I get over my embarrassment I shall discreetly ask someone. But it may take a while!

CHAPTER NINETEEN

PRESIDENTS, PHOTOGRAPHS
AND POLITICIANS

In the United States it is most unusual to get to meet the President personally. As a matter of fact, senators and congressmen are not too easily come by either unless you pay five hundred dollars or more a plate to attend a fund-raising dinner. This isn't because they want to remain aloof, it's just that it is such a huge country, with lots of people, that your chances of bumping into them are slim. This is different in Ireland as I have discovered to my absolute surprise and delight.

Shortly after I bought Barrow House I brought another small medical group to Ireland. We stayed as usual at the Ballygarry House Hotel, just outside Tralee. Now Owen McGillycuddy, the owner, is probably the smoothest, most professional hotel manager I have ever met. He has a lovely hotel but there is one little drawback which he is clever enough to turn into an asset.

He has a huge ballroom and function hall located under the accommodation area. Monday through Thursday it is possible to sleep undisturbed. But Friday, Saturday and Sunday there is usually some big party going on downstairs which means that, unless you have a good pair of ear plugs, you are not going to sleep until 4.30 am. So what does Owen do about this? It's simple. Anyone who stays in the hotel gets invited down to the party once the dinner speeches are over and the music begins. My groups just loved it as they got the opportunity to meet lots of Irish people and had one hell of a good time joining in the singing and dancing. Even the Americans who couldn't last until 4.30 am had a great time. After a few drinks and romps around the dance floor they went to bed in such an exhausted state that the Marine Corps Band could have come marching through and they wouldn't have heard it.

One Saturday morning Owen told us that if we went to the party that night, we would get to meet the Tánaiste, Dick Spring. At the time I knew very little about Irish politics and couldn't even pronounce Tánaiste let alone know what it stood for. When we found out that it was the equivalent of the vice-president or the deputy prime minister all the women in the group cancelled the sight-seeing trip for the day and we ran around worrying about our hair and what we were going to wear that night. Two went into town and bought new dresses. The rest of us switched and swopped around until we found something presentable.

We practised saying "Tánaiste" all day and made sure that our cameras would fit in our evening bags, so that we wouldn't look too gauche. When the time came to go downstairs, we looked a fine, handsome group with not a piece of chewing gum between the lot of us.

We went into the ballroom, which was darkly lit, the music had started and the dinner tables and chairs had been moved to the sides of the room. We found a table, sat down and looked around. Suddenly, we realised not one of us knew what Dick Spring looked like, nor could we get a clue who he was from looking at the people in the room. I saw Owen behind the bar and decided it was time for a consultation. I eased my way over to him, and not wanting anyone to hear me, because I felt foolish, leaned over, and said out of the corner of my mouth, "Owen, which one is he?"

Owen pointed him out. "Go over and introduce yourself," he said. Well, I didn't think I could do that at all as it might have seemed impolite. So I went back to our table and discreetly told everyone where to look. We all turned our heads, trying not to look obvious and not one of us had enough nerve to reach in our bags for our cameras. We didn't want to behave like tacky American tourists.

We kept him under surveillance long enough to observe that he was talking to everybody, and that the people around were just as relaxed with him as if he were "Joe Blow" from down the street. I suggested that we all go over and meet him and everyone said, "Oh no, we couldn't do that."

So then I said, "Well hell, I'm going to" and over I went to introduce myself. He smiled, looked me right in the eye, shook my hand and asked in a genuinely interested way what I was doing in Ireland. That is when I first fell in love with Dick Spring. When he told me he was from Tralee, I suddenly remembered my Auntie May in Boston. She grew up in Kerry and was always talking about a young relative of hers named Spring who was going to be a famous politician some day. In a flash it dawned on me that this was the person in front of me. He had absolutely no idea who my Auntie May was but he took a card out of his pocket and wrote a note on it for me to give to her. He then asked where the rest of my group was. I pointed out the table where they were sitting with their mouths wide open watching us, and he took me by the arm and walked over for me to introduce him.

You could have knocked us all down with feathers. He sat down at the table and talked to us all for at least twenty minutes. He knew that not one of us was a registered voter in Ireland or were ever likely to be. There were eighteen of us at that table and every one of us went back to the USA absolutely charmed and impressed with the Tánaiste of the Republic of Ireland. He was an incredible ambassador for his country, but it wasn't until later that we realised we had been so busy being impressed that we had forgotten to take photographs! But more about Dick Spring and Irish politics later. I have only told this part of the story to explain why I had the nerve to waylay the President of Ireland outside my driveway.

It started out as another beautiful sunny day in Ireland. The guests all had breakfast and I was pottering around in the front flower beds with the puppies who were trying to foil every attempt I made to tidy up the place. I noticed a car come down the driveway with two gentlemen in it. Ina came out of the big house and stopped to talk to them for a few minutes before they turned around and drove off. When I asked her who they were she just said with a shrug, "Oh, Special Branch" and walked off to the laundry room. Now Special Branch do not usually come down my driveway on a nice sunny day just to look at the scenery or pass the time of day with Ina. A thought had flashed through my mind. Oh God, what has Ina done now? But before I could question her further, I saw some motorcycle cops heading up the road towards the golf course. Then I saw all kinds of traffic activity and I realised that someone very important had to be playing golf that day.

Finally the curiosity got the best of me and I picked up the telephone, called the Golf Club and spoke to Mary O'Connor. I asked nonchalantly if anything special was going on that day. And she said, "Oh yes, we have our President playing here today."

I immediately said, "Oh my God, I have to get a photograph."

"Well, why don't you come up and meet him," she said. "He'll be in the club house in a few hours."

Just like that, "come up and meet the President." Simply didn't seem possible but it was Ireland and everything was possible.

So I grabbed Ina. We ran and washed our hair and changed our clothes, grabbed the camera and headed up to the club house. When we got there the place was crowded and the President was only on the twelfth tee. We sat there for a while and I realised that it was going to be a long time before the President got to the club house and crowds of people would be around him. Then it hit me. The President had to pass the end of my driveway when he was leaving. If I played my cards right, maybe I could get a photograph of him if I could just get his car to slow down.

I went looking for Peter Colleran, the manager of the golf club, and asked him if he had an Irish flag which I could borrow. He did. As we left the club house, I saw the President's motorcycle escort and went over to explain to them that I was going to take a photograph as they passed my driveway and not to shoot me as it would just be a camera I was holding. One guy looked at me and said, "Ma'am, don't worry, this is not the United States." I asked if they could just slow down a little so that I could get a better photograph and they told me they didn't know if they could, the President would be on a tight schedule to catch the ferry at Tarbert.

We went tearing back down to the house and grabbed some white chipboard, left over from the builders. We wrote "Hello President Hillary" in black paint. Then we headed up the driveway with our Stars and Stripes and the Tricolour. We put the chipboard sign up against a telephone pole across the road and draped the two flags over my guest house sign at the end of the driveway.

We had to make another trip down to the house for umbrellas, as it had started to rain and also get the leashes for the puppies as they had followed us and were determined not to be left out of the excitement. Allan wanted to know what we were up to. When we told him, he wasn't terribly impressed with our chances of getting a photograph but he agreed to mind the telephone for me anyway.

We sat there for what seemed to be hours in the wind and rain as the weather got nastier by the minute and people drove by looking at us strangely. But we both determined to see this through and even the puppies didn't grumble.

Then, at last, through a gap in the trees, we saw the motorcycle cops coming down the hill. I got the camera ready. A special branch car flashed past, then the motorcycles, then the President's car. They went so fast I didn't have time to rewind the film. All of a sudden, I heard brakes squeal and, believe it or not, the President's car came to a screeching halt. As I stood staring the door opened and out stepped President Paddy Hillery. He walked towards me with a big smile and his hand out. I was so dumb-struck that Ina had to push me forward. I had no idea what to do or say and then I realised I was soaking wet, my make-up long since washed off and blown away. In fact I looked a wreck. So what does old silver tongue say on meeting the President of Ireland? Yes, I said it, "Oh God, my hair is a mess." I couldn't believe I said it. I still can't believe I said it. I was so embarrassed that I blabbed away like even more of an idiot.

Fortunately Paddy Hillery is one of the most charming, gracious men whom God ever created and he took complete control of the situation. He asked his driver to get out of the car, handed my camera to him and asked him to take a photograph of us together. He then talked for a few moments, patted the puppies and excused himself so that he could catch the ferry.

We were so elated we ran down the driveway to tell Allan. Even he couldn't believe it as nothing like this could ever happen in the United States. A President getting out of his car, completely unprotected, to have his photograph taken with a complete stranger. Not only that but a dippy one who blabbered – totally unheard of.

Allan thought we were having him on but I told

him I had the evidence on film. He took the roll into town the next day and got it developed. When he came home he tossed the packet on the table between myself and Ina and said, "Well now I know why the President stopped. Firstly, he wanted to tell you how to spell his name correctly and then he saw you were flying the Stars and Stripes upside down which is the international distress signal."

We looked at the photographs in silence and sure enough we had his name spelt wrong. We had a fifty-fifty chance between an A or an E and we had blown it. And there as sure as God made little green apples was the Stars and Stripes flying upside down!

For a moment we felt a little put down because Allan was obviously gloating a little but then we bounced right back and decided that President Hillery was even more of a gentleman than we had thought because he hadn't said a word about our error. Just as we were getting on a roll again, laughing and enjoying the memory of a fantastic "happening," Allan gave us the final coup de grâce as he went out the door.

"That's probably why he left his sunglasses on, so he wouldn't be recognised."

We looked back at the photographs – sure enough he had his sunglasses on.

I had the photograph enlarged, framed and placed in a very conspicuous spot on the guest dining-room wall. A few days later Ina casually pointed out the photograph to some American guests. "Oh yes, that's the President of Ireland with myself and Maureen when he was here." Now she didn't say *he stayed* here but you know, and I know, that they thought he did and boy were they impressed. Another time when I heard her talking to some American guests about the photograph one of them asked in awe "Did he stay here?" I was at the far side of the diningroom and froze in my tracks waiting to hear if she was actually going to tell a "whopper". She looked at me briefly as if making up her mind and then seeing my look said, "Oh no, he was only up at the golf course for a quick game and could only stop by for a few minutes that day." These guests were even more impressed as it sounded as though the President was in the habit of stopping by frequently.

Now I am not above name-dropping but when I tell this story I tell the whole truth because I think it's very funny. Also I'm very proud a President of Ireland was such a gracious person and I like to brag to the whole world about it at any chance I get.

However, I have had some Irish guests who asked me, "Who is the man in the photograph?" and when I said, "Why, it's Paddy Hillery of course," the response was, "Well I knew he looked familiar but I didn't recognise him with his sunglasses on!"

I don't know if having the photograph on the wall of President Hillery went to our heads, but, not too long after that, I received a fax from Paris. The letterhead was impressive from a French government office on the Champs-Elysées. The fax read as follows:

"Dear Sir,

We are a group of five French men who will be touring your country with our President and wish to stay and play golf in Kerry for a few days – do you have accommodation available?"

I read the fax several times, looked back at the letterhead and thought, "Is it possible?" Then I read it again and thought, "Nah, not a hope." But I showed it to Allan and Marie just to see what their reaction would be. They responded initially the same way I had done but after we discussed it for a few minutes we decided that the fax probably referred to the president of their golf club.

The following Sunday I was absorbed in my usual routine of enjoying the Sunday newspapers, when I turned a page and there jumping out at me was a small headline which read, "French President to make private visit to Ireland!" I thought my heart would stop. My vision started to blur. The article said that the President had made several trips to Ireland in the past and planned as usual to spend a few days in his favourite county of all – Kerry!

I digested the article. The dates were the same as the reservation made by fax. I ran through the kitchen and out the back door screaming, "My God, we're getting Mitterand." By the time I got to Allan's office door, Marie was hard on my heels wondering what in the hell was going on and if she had heard me right.

I showed the two of them the article and their mouths dropped open. We then had a discussion about what on earth we were going to do. I opted for a total evacuation of the place and plane tickets to Florida. Allan and Marie were stunned that I should show such a cowardly streak. Marie assured me I would have no trouble being a gracious hostess to President Mitterand and that I could tell her all about it after he left because she had just remembered she wasn't going to be here on those dates. Allan tried to encourage me. He pointed out that I could get another photograph with a President for the wall. I swear he was already thinking of all his best French jokes.

Fortunately, there was only a week to wait. Which gave a relatively short time to panic but not enough time to do anything about it – like re-decorate the whole house! Marie and I kept trying to assure each other that it was just an incredible coincidence and that, of course, it would be so unlikely to have Mitterand as a guest. The thought of it was hilarious – but we didn't laugh too hard and there was a nervous edge to the sound. After all, this is Ireland and anything is possible.

The day of the expected arrival finally came. it wasn't that we believed there was a chance President Mitterand would come down the driveway, but the grounds were freshly mown, cut flowers from the garden were in every suite and I kept pacing in my new hairdo. I kept pacing because I didn't want to sit down and wrinkle my skirt. The afternoon seemed to last forever and still no sign of our French guests. I kept looking up the driveway. I tried not to show my anxiety in front of Marie but I noticed her eyes kept straying up there too. Allan was wandering around, humming the Marsellaise, the rendition of which indicated further practice would have been well in order.

Then all of a sudden a big shiny new car, with five men in it, pulled up at the top of the driveway and stopped. Marie saw it first and let out a warning yelp that brought Allan and me running to the window where she was. As we stared with bated breath, two men got out of the car and opened the trunk. We couldn't see what they were doing but, when they closed the trunk, they seemed to be carrying something as they came around to the front of the car. We watched the scene unfold. Marie was the first to break the silence. She shrugged her shoulders and said as she walked off, "Bet a tenner that's not Mitterand." I didn't take the bet. I felt she was probably right as it was most unlikely that a French President would ride down my driveway seated on the hood of a car swigging a can of beer!

These were our French guests all right. They were so much fun, we took photographs of them anyway – even if Mitterand wasn't in the group! Oh well, at least we hadn't told the neighbours and the next photograph I got was much more special than the missed chance of one with a French President anyway.

I've already told you that I had been totally impressed with Dick Spring when I met him the first time. When I started to follow Irish politics, it didn't take me long to realise that my first impressions had been right. My Auntie May didn't just have a nice relative – he was blooming smart also. I have never been crazy about Labour Party politicians. When I was a young teenager in England the only channel on television on Friday night was a political discussion programme which went out from 9 pm onwards. The Labour Party MPs, Michael and Dingle Foote, debated representatives from Tory and Liberal parties for one solid hour on current issues, when we could have had something interesting, such as *I love Lucy*.

Television was so new at the time that we watched anything including the test patterns. But Michael and Dingle were too much for me. The only pleasure I got from their programme had been sneering at Michael's awful tie and hornrimmed glasses, calling him a "Commie," and swearing that when I grew up I would never vote Labour.

Oh well, as they say in politics, never say never and if I could vote in Ireland, Dick Spring would probably be my man, even though he does head up the Labour Party. Irish politics has to qualify as a blood sport. Observing it is like watching American football where you pick your favourite team of players, watch them go into the huddle where the quarter-back calls the play and, once the ball gets snapped and the play goes into motion, every mean son of a bitchin' bruiser from the other side comes crashing across the line to kill, maim and mutilate and stop anyone from gaining a yard. It's definitely a tough game and it was hard for me to understand after reading the biographies of Daniel O'Connell, Parnell and Redmond, why anyone would want to be a politician in Ireland.

At first standing on the outside looking in, I thought Irish politics had to be the ultimate call to bravery, altruism or sheer bravado. There were also times when I looked at the Irish political system and thought, "Oh God, this is how Huey Long ran Louisiana." Just as I thought that, darn if the government hadn't fallen in a way that couldn't have happened in Louisiana.

I think the Irish electorate is probably the most fiercely independant and, in its own way, sophisticated electorate any politician could hope to deal with. It's almost as though there's an unspoken agreement to "keep the buggers on their toes" by voting in such a way as to continually force a coalition government.

The whole thing reminds me of a story I read about a major Ivy League University in the US. An alumnus had written to the admissions office on behalf of his son's application. In his letter he said something to the effect that, while the young man was not an outstanding athlete or first in his class, and he probably would never be a great leader of men, he was a sound, solid all-rounder who would be an asset to the university. The head of the admissions committee immediately replied "This Fall, according to the letters from students requesting admission, we have approximately two thousand leaders arriving on campus – please send your son immediately as we will desperately need a follower." Every Irishman seems to be a leader so it's harder than hell to find followers.

Ireland is a country which is legendary for brilliance and eloquence. Yet a lot of the politicians whom I have listened to seem to spend a lot of effort trying not to offend anyone. They use fifty thousand words to say nothing and thus end up insulting everyone. Worse still they copy each other. And if a new form of description is used by one at the beginning of the week, nearly everyone is using it by the end. And they use it over and over and over . . . and oh God, over again as if there was safety and security in repetition. For the last number of years, everything has been "on course", "on train", "on stream" and the poor lads must be continually working late because everything is summed up, "at the end of the day."

I shall probably never understand the political scene in Ireland. But that doesn't stop me from having my favourite politicians, and beyond a doubt, Dick Spring is one of them. I've got my other favourites and I certainly don't confine my choices to specific political parties but, when Dick stands up to speak, he stands straight and tall, not a bit like a nervous football quarter-back listening for footsteps behind him.

As you can probably guess, the next photograph for my wall was of Dick Spring at Barrow House and I have Eric and my wonderful Australian group from Melbourne to thank for that. Eric's group issued a tournament challenge to the captain of the Tralee club and, after Eric sent a list of names and short biographical sketches of his team members, there wasn't a moment's hesitation about taking up the offer. Good Lord, I looked at the list myself and wondered why Alan Bond wasn't on it. Unless of course, they had decided to exclude him.

When the Australian group played their tournament against the Tralee club, the home team did us proud and fielded a group that would make any Irishman burst with pride. The Australians had made arrangements for everyone to come down to a "barbie" at Barrow House afterwards and Dick Spring was part of the group from the golf club.

I had missed my chance once before. So I was absolutely shameless and pounced at the first opportunity to have my photograph taken with him to send to Auntie May. And darn if he wasn't even more handsome, charming and gracious than the first time I had met him. I called Auntie May in Boston later that evening to tell her all about it and she explained again how she was related to him. Her grandmother had been Mary Spring, a sister of Dick's great-great-grandfather, which would make the grandmother Dick's great-great-aunt and Lord knows how many cousins removed from Auntie May, but a cousin none the less. It wasn't exactly a close relationship, but enough for Auntie May as she came from a very small family and had very few relatives to call her own. She was so short of relations that she'd told me that she and I were related but that it was "under the blanket."

When she first told me this when I was small, I had no idea what "under the blanket" meant. When I was old enough to know, I asked her "how" and "who". I was most curious about the whole thing by then. But although I asked the question many times, she always brushed me off with, "Oh, it was a long time ago and I'm not sure I have it straight enough to tell the details, but you *are* related to me." That had been the end of it.

But it hadn't been the end of it because one evening many, many years later, when I was happily telling Auntie May about the cook-out and the photograph with Dick Spring, she had said, "Well, you know, you're related to him too." I was stunned and asked her how this was so. She then explained "I've always told you that you and I were related under the blanket. My grandmother always said . . . " And she proceeded to give me the full rundown.

Well it's like this: Great-Great-Aunt Mary spilled the beans a long time ago without any idea where it would be repeated seventy-five years later and Dick had just got himself another cousin – ME. When I asked Auntie May why she had never told me before, she said, "Well I was always going to tell you when you were older." Good grief, I was already fifty-two years old – how much longer was she going to wait if I hadn't called that night? The incident involving a romp under the blanket had to have occurred close to two hundred years before and was hardly anything I'd worry about the neighbours knowing. The story had been old when Great-Great-Aunt Mary first told it. Besides, if one of my great-grandmothers, back down the long line of ancestry, had chosen to mess around, at least she had good taste!

Yes, I have President Hillery's photograph on the dining-room wall and I still give Ina my look when I hear her imply that he stayed here. But I also have Dick's photograph up there. When a guest recognises him from newspapers or CNN, I furtively look around to make sure Ina won't catch me before I casually say, "Oh yes, a cousin of mine you know." It could only happen in Ireland and I can't help but wonder if there's anything else Auntie May has to tell me when I'm old enough, but I'm sure as hell not going to ask.

CHAPTER TWENTY

YOU KNOW WHO

From the very beginning when I was first aware that, yes indeed, I had a ghost, it never occurred to me to give him a name. I honestly didn't feel that I needed to give him one as I felt sure he had his own. It wasn't as though we had been formally introduced. We were getting along just fine without needing to be on a first name basis. I always just referred to him as "himself" or "you know who." But within a week of Ina's arrival she had named him Séamus. I was a little annoyed about this as he was my ghost. I felt that if he was going to be given a name I should have at least been consulted. But Séamus he became and I have had no indication from him that he is displeased with the choice.

I have already explained that everyone in the neighbourhood already knew there was a ghost at Barrow House before I bought the place. But what no one in the area seems to know is that Séamus is a very nice, pleasant and playful fellow. He doesn't go around scaring people by jumping out of closets or clanking chains at night. Well, there was *one* occasion when he kicked up a little fuss but even then it was doubtful whether he was the guilty party.

Although I had heard some bad reports about his previous behaviour, I had no reason to believe one bit of it. Either everything had been blown out of proportion, or Séamus had become a reformed ghost. His past wasn't significant to me and, as far as I was concerned, he started out with a completely clean slate and for the most part he has kept it so. What really annoyed me was that so many people in the area were unwilling to give Séamus the benefit of the doubt or even a second chance.

Everyone who had worked at Barrow House had done so with their ears filled with all kinds of nonsense about my ghost before they even started their first day's work. Now I know this sounds as though I am being as blindly defensive about Séamus as a mother would be about her child but, in my case, that was simply not true. Whenever the neighbours said my kids had done something, they usually had and were guilty up to their eyeballs. But I was convinced that Séamus was a victim of malicious gossip. It's just as well for some that Séamus is a very gentle ghost or the reprisals could be horrible for those who have slandered him.

Before the first guest arrived, I did realise that Séamus could be a bit of a PR problem. I thought long and hard about whether I should admit to anyone other than Ina that, yes, indeed, Barrow House had a ghost. By then I had been around Séamus for some time and felt confident enough that he would never let the side down, unless he was extremely provoked.

Also, and this is a very important point, there was a very warm comforting sense of peace at Barrow House which everyone noticed. That would be proof enough that no evil lingered here.

I decided that I simply could not, if asked, deny Séamus's presence. I mean, come on, if someone wants to stay in an old house they surely had to realise that there was a chance of a ghost, and when it's one like Séamus they should consider themselves fortunate not to be charged extra for the privilege.

That was my logic. And the first people who stayed in the big house were a group of three English men who were delivering our company cars from England before the start of the first guest season. They arrived late from the ferry at Rosslare on a wild and windy April night. The night was pitch black, and the trees and shrubs swayed round and round as they fumbled in the dark for our boathouse door. After I warmed them up with tea and a hot snack, I took them over to the main house to show them where they were to sleep. All three were well over six feet tall and fine strapping men. Of course, the finest of them all was my delightful Brendan Kehoe, a second generation Irishman from Wexford whom I had adopted unconditionally after having met him in England when we were buying the cars.

When one of his two associates entered the front hallway, he asked, "You don't have a ghost, do you?" I thought he was joking. "Of course we do," I said, "and he's going to be very upset that the bunch of you are stomping around at this time of night, keeping him awake." Only two of them showed up for breakfast the next morning. Brendan explained that, as soon as I left, the one who asked about the ghost had gone sixty miles an hour up the driveway, headed for town!

So much for openness. I discussed it with Allan and Ina and we decided that maybe we should be a little more discreet about the information we divulged. Actually the two of them told me to keep my big mouth shut. I did very well for a while, let's face it, we were not exactly inundated with guests.

But then we had other guests who asked about a ghost. Actually it was Marie and Wally from Roscrea who, the following year, tried to teach us about training Paddy's biting habits.

This was the first time they stayed. Wally had gone off to the golf course after a late breakfast, leaving Marie, Ina and myself in the diningroom chatting away. As the morning turned into afternoon we took out a bottle of port with stilton cheese and crackers and really got talking. Marie said how beautiful the house was and how peaceful and tranquil the whole place seemed. Then she said, "I was wondering at first if you had a ghost, but I didn't get any vibrations and there's such a lovely feeling. It just wouldn't be possible to have a ghost here. I can always tell a house that has a ghost, I feel the coldness just engulfing me."

Ina and I didn't look at each other. We just kept smiling, nodding our heads and listening. Marie went on to tell us about her friend in Cornwall who had an old house with a very nasty ghost who shoved people and knocked things out of their hands. Then she said, "Last night I heard a noise and at first I thought it was a ghost, but then I realised it was just the central heating coming on."

Ina and I looked at each other quickly. We don't have central heating!

When Marie left to go upstairs Ina said, "You'd better have a talk with Séamus and tell him noises in the night are simply not on." I asked her why didn't she go and tell him off herself and she said, "Sure he'd mind you better than me. You own the place and you've known him longer."

When Marie went for a walk, I climbed the stairs to the second floor and passed on the request for no noises in the night, please. Now this is when I found out that Séamus my dog and Séamus my ghost have a lot in common. They get petulant and sulk. When I came downstairs to the kitchen and dining-room, every time I turned a light switch on, the bulb blew. I called Billy O'Sullivan, my electrician, to check as I was convinced we had a short circuit of some kind but he could find nothing wrong. None of the new light bulbs he put in for me blew when he turned on the switch. As he was leaving he told me that there was absolutely nothing wrong with my wiring or sockets, he had no explanation for what had happened. His parting line was "I dunno, they either were all bad bulbs or it must have been your ghost."

Well, of course, it was my ghost and he was cheesed off. He had been accused of making noises in the night when he hadn't done it at all. I climbed up the stairs again and apologised to him but I made sure I didn't touch a light switch until I had apologised. Those darn bulbs were expensive.

I have discovered over the years that the light bulbs and Allan's stereo are Séamus's favourite means of communication. His light bulb trick is the only really aggravating thing that he does. Thank heavens. That little trick is expensive enough. All of our guests with the exception of the English guy enjoy Séamus being around. Even the ones who refuse to believe in him have a good laugh. Some guests absolutely swear that he has hidden their spare pair of socks or swiped their toothpaste but no one has ever had anything to report which wasn't good-natured and pleasant.

Marie Ferris, a very lovely lady who worked in Barrow House for a while, would get upset with him occasionally. She swore he moved her cleaning supplies around and messed with the curtains. Marie is the most organised lady I have ever met in my life and certainly was not going to let her routine be interfered with by anyone, let alone a ghost. She scolded Séamus something awful and he soon learned who not to mess with. But he did have to do something every so often, just to let her know he was still around and not *completely* intimidated. But he was always smart enough, when dealing with Marie, to make his games few and far between and to run to ground immediately.

So do I talk about Séamus to the guests and everyone who works here? Absolutely. After all, it isn't as though I'm hiding a blood-crazed gorilla in the attic. Besides, as I have already told you, all my staff had heard about him long before they ever came to work here and I've had some guests tell me at breakfast that they had heard all about my ghost the night before at a local pub. Fortunately it was no surprise to them and the pub conversation was usually humorous and good natured. However, I do have one old crab in the neighbourhood who claims to have seen Séamus and has nothing good to say about him, atall, atall. This old crab has nothing good to say about anyone and, between you and me, I have no idea if Séamus had had enough and was settling some accounts or whether it was just another night when the face was in the brandy. I would love to think that Séamus had scared the hell out of the vicious old crab. But it would be contrary to his dignified, gentle nature and, alas I think it was the brandy. But I can always hope!

Ever since I pooh-poohed the ghost stories told to

me in the past about Barrow House, nobody bothers to tell them to me anymore. So I have no idea what the current stories are. One of the old ones was about a man who worked for the county on the roads. He took shelter from a thunderstorm some time during the years the house was vacant. Just as he was shaking himself off to get dry, he looked up and saw the ghost and promptly took off running. He jumped over a wall, broke both his legs but still managed to run the three miles to Fenit. I am not even going to make a snide remark about anyone working for the county road department having that much energy. All I'll say to that story is if anyone believes it – I've got a bridge in Brooklyn I'd like to talk to them about.

CHAPTER TWENTY-ONE

THE BUILDERS

"Out of the depths have I called unto thee, O Lord:
Lord, hear my voice."
Psalm 130.

The De Profundis is a Latin prayer written by St.
Thomas Aquinas, based on one of King David's
psalms from the Old Testament. I strongly suspect
that the inspiration for this psalm came to King David
when he was building the temple in Jerusalem. I
highly recommend it now for anyone dealing with
Irish workmen or builders. As a matter of fact it has
been most appropriate for me as I learned that prayer
in my early days as the result of my first involvement
with an Irish scam. As a child I was told by a kindly
Irish nun that if I read that prayer ten times a day for
thirty days I would go to Heaven regardless of
whatever terrible sin was on my soul.

I was only ten years old at the time, but I still knew
a good deal when I heard one. Although I wasn't

exactly planning a life of crime and evil, I decided that I would be foolish not to cover my odds with an insurance policy of thirty days of prayer. I read that whole thing ten times a day for thirty days. That was a miserable chore for a ten-year-old. When I finished my very last line I went running to the nun to let her know that I was now assured of Heaven.

To my horror, she told me she couldn't remember having told me to read it only ten times a day, as she was sure that it was supposed to be thirty times a day for thirty days!

No, I didn't start over. For the rest of my life, every time I have read about someone blowing themselves up in a car bomb for an instant trip to heaven, or marching into battle, convinced that bullets wouldn't hurt them, I just know that somewhere in the background is the equivalent of a little Irish nun who screwed up the instructions.

However, all was not lost, and my time was not wasted. Whenever I have been in a desperate situation, the first lines of that prayer have come instantly to mind. Actually, if that Irish nun was right about the thirty times for thirty days, after twenty-eight years of working in hospitals and eight years dealing with Irish workmen and builders, I am home free if God just counts lines instead of expecting me to remember the whole thing. For the times I have raised my eyes to Heaven and pleaded "Out of the depths I cry to Thee O Lord" have been so numerous that if the lines don't count, the suffering surely should!

Now most people have heard Ireland called the land of Saints and Scholars, which was probably perfectly true as a description at one time. But that time was long ago, and really needs to be updated. It took me a while to figure out what happened. But apparently, over one thousand years ago, the Vikings came to pillage and plunder, and either killed all the saints, or chased them off to Europe, where they founded large monasteries with EU funds and never wrote home. The saints who survived here did so by hiding and have only been known to surface on rare occasions ever since. And the scholars – well most of them now work for the newspapers, mostly the *Sunday Independent* and, if some politicians were able to wield the same axe as the Vikings, we wouldn't be seeing much of the scholars either.

Now, as for the Vikings, after they pillaged and plundered, they decided to stay, and settle down, and continue their professional careers in assorted business ventures, but mostly they concentrated on the building and contracting trade, and car hire companies at Dublin and Shannon airports!

I have not yet told you about Barrow House and Irish builders. I was going to wait until it was far enough in the past so that I could see the humour in it. But it is unlikely that I shall live another hundred years, so I've decided I might as well get on with it now, and at least, if nothing else, wreak some revenge.

Voltaire said that the pen is mightier than the sword. Take my word, I would very much have preferred to use the sword on many occasions in my dealings with these Vikings. I just didn't have a sword handy when I needed it, and now, eight years later, doubt that I can afford one, as the bastards have got all my money!

Before I go any further I feel I must explain that I am not writing anything an Irish person wouldn't write themselves if they thought there was any point. Most of my Irish friends and neighbours, or strangers met on trains, can either top any story I may have to tell about the building trade, or at least equalise it.

The thing to remember about a Viking bandit is that he is not selective about his victims and will "Do" anyone. Some foreigners who have built in Ireland have got their backs up because they thought the treatment they received was especially reserved for them. This is simply not so. Anyone on these shores with as little as a penny in their pocket is considered, in a phrase borrowed from elsewhere, "a legitimate target."

Oh yes, every country has their chancers, cowboys and crooks, but the thing about the Irish ones is that they are so damn good at it. There isn't a fighting chance of winning. If you have any sense at all, you save your energy to concentrate on damage limitation to your bank account. If you have a shirt to your back at the end of the day, you have to learn to be grateful. There are many before who went cold in the winter, until they could recoup the price of a piece of cloth to cover their bodies.

When I decided to renovate Barrow House, I knew that I was at a severe disadvantage. One, I didn't live here, and two, I didn't have the slightest idea of what I was doing. Other than that I also had the problem that I was a blonde female with an atrocious Southern accent, married to an American doctor, and had all the characteristics of a well-fed golden goose ripe for the plucking. In actual fact I was just a gosling, without a feather to lose, and the last thing I needed was to lay an egg!

After thinking long and hard, I came to the conclusion that I would divide the whole project up into segments so that, if I felt I had been taken at any point, I could at least make it self-limiting. I also told my first builder that my philosophy was if you are going to rob me, do it well the first time, because you are not going to get a second chance. So he did!

There were also other problems, apart from the consensus that I had a bottomless pit where I kept my money. Without a doubt, Irish builders are male chauvinists who are convinced that women do not really know what they want, and that it is part of their responsibility as a builder to tell them the way it should be. Couple that with the fact that most of the construction people I was involved with didn't like old buildings and would much rather build new and modern. It's easy to see that the path to conflict was already there before the first day's work.

I had some smaller projects done on the boat-house apartment before I started on the main house.

And because it was going to cost a great deal of money, I was going to get several estimates. Now I had no quarrel with the man who did the boathouse apartment, until he became very unpleasant and overbearing because I was going to get estimates for the rest of the work. His estimate was much higher than the others, but if it had been the lowest, I doubt that I would have given him the job, as I didn't care for his chauvinistic attitude. Hell, I didn't know at the time that they're all like that!

My next builder was a delightful young man. But, my God, what a chauvinist for one so young. Every time I explained how I wanted something done, he would reply, "No, no, not at all, not at all, you wouldn't want to do it that way at all." When I asked him why, he would have at least six reasons. When I was a hospital administrator I was used to gathering other people's opinions, and weighing them, but the final decision and responsibility was always mine. I did with this man what I have always done in the organisations I have worked with. That is to give every respect to opinions, but if I was to make a different decision I would always explain why, as I did not want to close off channels of communication among my assistants. I would go back to my young builder and say, "I have thought over what you have said, and I really appreciate what you have to say, but taking everything into consideration I still want to do it this way." But dammit if he didn't come up with six more reasons why it shouldn't be done that way.

This would go on and on over every little thing. And then one day I was very tired, and I just didn't want to go through any big long diplomatic foray. I just wanted to get the damn thing done my way. In my weariness I came up with a brilliant flash of inspiration. I said, "I am quite sure you are absolutely right, but my husband wants it done this way." And, do you know what my lovely young gentleman said. He said, "And sure isn't he absolutely right!" I felt like punching him out on the spot. If I had been twenty years younger, I would have done, but age, fortunately, makes us a little craftier. During the next few months the work sailed along brilliantly. Whenever there was a problem or conflict, I would talk sorrowfully about my husband's wishes. When, all the time, my husband was in Florida, and didn't have a clue what was going on in Barrow House.

This worked fine until we retired and Allan spent time around the place, enough for it to be obvious just who was making the decisions about what was to be done with the house. Then, of course, it was back to long debates. But by that time most of the initial work had been done anyway. I wasn't going to do anything more until the following year. One of the reasons for this was that I was just as tired and worn out with workmen as my bank balance was!

This was when I discovered another characteristic of Irish workmen – they never finish the job, and no one ever finishes paying for it. Let me explain how that works. As soon as I announced that the next stage of renovation was to be the outbuildings, and that I was not going to start on them until the following spring, we settled our account and it was explained to me that the few odds and ends left to do would be finished over the next few weeks. Well, some of them did get done in the next few months, but then he came around to collect for those same odds and ends which should have been included in the original price. When I questioned this, I forget exactly what the explanation was. It was such a long piece of bullshit that it was easier to pay up than listen to more.

When I asked about the other items to be done I was told not to worry, they would be finished up when they were doing the next stage. I wasn't to worry my head one bit. Ha! When the next project was almost completed, it was the same story all over again. The job not finished but payment demanded, and then back in another few months for another whip around and still the darn work not finished.

I honestly don't know which was the more aggravating, the money or the bullshit, or the knowledge that I couldn't possibly win. I have one set of swinging doors between the guest dining room and the kitchen, which were supposed to swing back and forth, like the old western saloon doors. But mine only swing out. I was assured by one of my builders that absolutely nowhere in Ireland could be found hinges which would allow a door to swing back and forth. When I exclaimed, "Bullshit, are you telling me that they can't even be made?" I received a frosty look. Roughly translated it meant "Look lady, no matter what you say those are the damn doors you are getting!"

I could go on and on with this tale of woe, but I will just content myself with recounting the highlights. My special favourites, like the master switch I wanted in the guest dining-room and kitchen area, so that I could turn out all the lights at one time when closing up the place at night. I got it as requested, but it is located in the hallway, right next to the bathroom door. So, when a diner is unobtrusively trying to use the bathroom, he draws attention to himself when he thinks he is turning on the bathroom light. It takes him a little while to understand that the sudden silence in the dining room is not because everyone has gone quiet to hear him pee, but because he has pitched the whole damn place into darkness. In that same bathroom, the electric shower was mounted in the shower cubicle, but had no water supply provisioned in the wall. The shower head in my own new bathroom was solidly fixed at an angle, so, when it was turned on, it sprayed the shower curtain flat against the ceiling and drenched the sink, commode, and far wall without putting a drop of water on my body.

My absolute favourite, and the episode that reduced me to a screaming, babbling idiot, was my gate. It was to be made and installed from the side of the boathouse to the sea wall. It was explained to me that this gate would have to be specially made to order. Obviously, from the price of it, I was going to have the skills of the greatest craftsman in Ireland. All kinds of measurements were made, and two weeks later the gate arrived accompanied by the workmen to install it. I looked at the gate and was suitably impressed, and then went on to busy myself in the kitchen, preparing the evening dinner for the guests.

Allan came in shortly after and asked me if I had seen the gate, and I told him yes. He asked me if I didn't think it was a little big, and I told him that it looked fine to me, and went on scraping the new potatoes. A little while later, Allan came into the kitchen again and said, "I really think you need to take a look at this" and led me out to the side of the building. My workmen were moving the two sections of the gate around, trying to fit them. My husband said, "Don't they look too wide for that space?" The lead guy said "No, no, not at all, when we get the metal fixtures on the walls, they'll slide in for a perfect fit."

They did look a little too wide to me but he was so convincing that I went back to scraping my potatoes, and my husband gave up trying to warn me that all was not well.

About fifteen minutes later I heard a horrendous screeching noise, and went running. I could not believe what I saw. The stone post built into the sea wall, which had been there for at least two hundred years, was missing. The screeching noise was the valiant workmen using a circular rotating power blade on the side of my two hundred year old boathouse wall to carve out room for the gate to fit into. I looked over the sea wall, and there was my stone post in pieces lying ten feet down there in the tide. I looked back at what had been the old wall of the boat house, and there was a strange curvature which centuries of wind, gales or Cromwell certainly had not produced. And there was my gate, obviously a good foot too wide for the space, and they were trying to make room for it by knocking out my sea wall and cutting off part of my boathouse. I lost it, I screamed, I yelled, I jumped up and down and what was worse, every time I started to run out of steam, I looked at these workmen, and they were just staring at me, completely unaware that they had one damn bit to do with my hysterical behaviour, and I started off screaming and yelling again. Finally my husband contacted my builder on his mobile phone, and he arrived in time to haul off the gate and the workmen before I committed mayhem.

After that episode I decided to lie low for a while and restrain myself from starting any more projects. I desperately needed the break and I kept remembering the saying, "If you swim with sharks, you're going to get eaten." So I decided to limit my time in the water and paddle like hell for dry land.

But Barrow House and Séamus, my ghost, are hard taskmasters, and it wasn't long before I was walking and pacing looking at all the things I wanted to do. It was then that I went soft in the head. I am embarrassed to admit it now but I'll do it anyway. I wanted to do what no Irishman I knew of had done before. I wanted to win in a building project, and my arrogance set me up for the greatest come-uppance a supposedly halfway intelligent lady could hope to have. I hired an architect.

Now, I have no excuse for this insanity. I cannot claim ignorance. Before I even spent a penny on renovating Barrow House, I received a letter in Florida from an Irish architectural firm, who sought me out and offered their professional services. I had lunch with their man, and got a bill for twelve hundred pounds. What's worse I paid for the damn lunch. I should have known better, but my brain was weak and fragile and my arrogance got in the way. And yes, after that incredible experience with an architect, I actually went back for more, but at least it was a different one, and I didn't buy lunch!

The work I wanted done was to be the last stage of the renovation of the outbuildings. The boathouse had already been completed, which left the stables, coach house and old milking shed to be resurrected from their derelict state. I really did not want to get involved in such a large project but I simply could not help myself. Every evening in the summer time when I took my walk around the grounds, my eyes were drawn to those buildings and I could visualise what they would look like. I drew all kinds of floor plans and changed my mind a hundred times. While I was doing that I was safe. It was only when I finally had together what I wanted that I stepped over into dangerous territory – I wanted a thatched roof!

Once I saw that thatched roof in my mind's eye, all my little scratched floor plans fell together and nothing could stop me or save me. I do believe that Séamus my ghost and the little people had struck again. Before I bought Barrow House, I had never any desire to build or renovate anything with the exception of my little cottage across the bay. Yes, I had been involved in major building programmes in hospitals but that had been totally different and should have surely made me even more reluctant to ever put one brick on top of another.

Allan was right when he had observed that from the very beginning I didn't own Barrow House. It owned me, all of me including my heart and soul and bloody bank account and even had me as a daily slave catering to its every need or whim.

But I couldn't help myself because I had surrendered as a willing slave a long time before. I had also accepted all the consequences because the personal rewards of pleasure, joy and sense of accomplishment were far greater than anything I had ever previously experienced. When I walked down the driveway or around the grounds and looked at the place, it was the first time in my life that I could see something so tangible as a result of my hard work, enthusiasm and commitment. It was like a drug and totally addictive. I had to renovate the outbuildings and I had to have a thatched roof!

Of course Séamus and the little people were involved in this decision because the very next week's edition of *The Kerryman* newspaper had a photograph and an article about a young woman from the area who had just completed a year long thatching course sponsored by the Irish government. The government had initiated the programme to re-introduce the art of thatching in a country where the skill had almost died out because there were so few thatched roofs left. They were also giving grants to home owners to restore old roofs where thatch had been replaced with a more modern covering. I didn't want their grant but, Lord above, I did want their thatcher and joy to the world, she was a female and she would be my revenge on Irish workmen.

I immediately called the newspaper for the telephone number but they could only give me a rural address. So the following Sunday I roamed the wilds of the North Kerry countryside tracking down my thatcher somewhere around Upper and Lower Moyvane where there are lots of farmhouses with dogs that would eat you just for a snack. I was finally successful and, as soon as I set eyes on Mairead Hanrahan and heard her speak, I knew she was perfect for the job – she was.

I applied for planning permission in August and expected to receive it in two months – I didn't. In four months I still hadn't got it and when I complained, a strange woman lurked around the place. She even climbed over my back wall to check a Barrow House sign which I had had taken down for the winter. My gardener watched her in disbelief. He had no idea who she was. But light was shed on the mystery when I received a letter from Kerry County Council a few days later informing me that I was only allowed two signs for advertising purposes unless I had planning permission.

I finally got planning permission in April which was too late to start renovations since the guest season was about to start. So the whole project had to be re-scheduled. Instead of the thatched roof being the last part, it was started in August while the rest of the work would start in late September to be completed by Christmas. This meant Allan and I could not escape to the sunshine until the first of the year when everything was finished.

Well actually it didn't work out like that at all, which shouldn't have been surprising. By the middle of November my beautiful lawn and flower beds were mud. I wasn't speaking to my architect. And the stables and coach house had looked better when they were derelict. However, I did have a beautiful thatched roof, for all the good it did me. Two weeks later Leo, my builder, announced that he would be knocking off for Christmas and New Year and would be back without a problem sometime in early January – maybe!

Then the storms and gales came and Allan

suggested we use the time to get to hell out of the country while we could. When he asked me where I wanted to go, I didn't think twice – "Jerusalem," I said. When he asked me why, I told him that I needed to talk to God and that had been His last known address on earth as far as I knew. I was definitely getting close to the edge!

So we went to Israel and I looked in awe at the Holy City. When we went to the Wailing Wall in the old section of the city, I was just a little tempted to write a note to God with some reference to my wretched Irish building projects. But I didn't – it was such a reverent and holy place, I didn't feel it would have been appropriate. I do have to confess that when we were in Masada, I did look around and wonder where they had got their builders from. In the old Arab quarter, I found the most beautiful hand painted ceramic tiles which would cover over a glaring error in an outer wall height. That error was why I wasn't speaking to my architect. Hell, I couldn't speak to him. When I saw the wall I was too angry to be able to get my teeth unclenched. It's funny though how prayers can be answered. I had been hoping for the wall to shrink but in Jerusalem I had found a way to just make it *look* as though it had.

We returned to Ireland and began the terrible winter of our discontent. We were knee deep in mud and, to top it off, a winter storm blew in with gusts up to one hundred and ten miles per hour and had taken part of the boathouse roof off again and flooded the basement of the big house.

I had sodden boxes of papers and records which had to be saved and even though my first inclination was just to dump them over the sea wall and head for Shannon airport while I had one thread of sanity left, I couldn't do it because I had no clean clothes – at least none that I could find as we also had had no electricity for two days and besides I couldn't find my passport.

So I stayed and started salvaging what I could of the sodden boxes. And as I did so I started to read the faxes I had sent to friends in the USA and the notes I had left on the fridge door every evening for Ina. The humour started to come back.

Being an optimist is not always easy and sometimes takes conscienciously hard effort and believe you me, that winter of my discontent, it would have been less effort to reach for the gun, the rope or to jump the sea wall into the tide. But dammit, I've never fired a gun in my life and don't like loud noises. I have a fear of heights and the tide was never in when I needed it. Besides I am far too good a swimmer to let myself drown and would have just ended up treading water until the tide went out and beached me. Then I would have looked like a right idiot walking home and would probably have caught my death from pneumonia, which would have served me right.

Besides, there are some things I do well and despair is not one of them so instead I read my old faxes and started to laugh. I had absolutely no control of the building project, the mud or the relentless rain. My apartment was a wreck with pots and buckets everywhere to catch the water from the leaking ceiling. My dogs were sodden and smelly and hibernating on the couch and armchairs because the rugs were too wet. Allan was huddled in a dry corner with a bath towel over his head and a blanket around him to keep warm. The wild look in his staring eyes told me not to even consider asking him if he was all right or he would reach for an axe. It wasn't just the building project and my bank balance that was out of control. Hell, at that point it seemed that my whole life was out of control.

So what did I do? I gathered up my sodden papers, went into my office, took out a fresh notepad and started to write. At least something was back in order because the pen and paper were under my control. As I wrote, nothing else mattered as spring would come, our new living quarters would be finished, the dogs would be dry, the insurance would cover the damage, the frantic wild look in Allan's eyes would bloom and glow in the sunshine and I could end up a famous author, or at least a sane innkeeper. I wrote every day and it was the most wonderful therapy. I was so engrossed I didn't hear the wind and rain beating at the windows and roof. I didn't see the mud because I didn't go outside. And when my builder, Leo, came up to ask a question or announce the latest financial disaster, I simply snarled at him for the interruption and told him that I didn't give a damn. He should just do what needed to be done and I'd see it in the spring.

And it worked because spring finally came with a glorious burst of joy, with green buds and wild flowers and I had six chapters of a book written. The construction showed some reasonable semblance of being completed within this century and at least my new living quarters were ready for occupancy. Well they were, apart from rain damage to the new carpeting because the windows and doors had been put in back to front and one of the fireplaces belched smoke. Other than that, the place was wonderful and a luxurious improvement over the boathouse apartment, which, after the trials and tribulations of that awful winter, almost resembled the living conditions of Bangladeshi squatters in the monsoon season.

But it was over. Spring had arrived, there were multiple reservations for the coming season, we had a lovely new place to live, including "his" and "her" bathrooms with dressing rooms, the dogs had their own bedroom with doggie door to the outside and the bluebells were just waiting to bloom. "Out of the depths." I had come, oh Lord.

As the lawn grew back and the outside painting and whitewashing was completed, the whole place became more and more beautiful. And when my Jerusalem tiles were put in place, the whole thing wasn't just beautiful – it was a bloody work of art.

So yes, of course, I forgave every scoundrel who was ever involved. How could I be upset when it all turned out so well? And when each new group of guests exclaim at how beautiful Barrow House is, I make sure that I show them the old photographs so that they can really be impressed. They "ooh" and "aah" with wonderment at the transformation and ask me how I ever managed to do it. I try to look suitably humble and modest. And cross my fingers behind my back, try hard not to watch the ceiling and mumble something to the effect of "Aw shucks t'weren't nothing to it"!

"T'weren't nothing to it" – some of those blighters almost did me in. However, God's eyes have not been turned against me for my architect has built his house and to all popular accounts his roof leaks like a sieve. And as for the others – well thanks to my parents, the blood in my veins is one hundred percent Kerry female which means that even if my body was broken and I was bleeding to death, I'd be damn certain to get the last word. Thank you, Voltaire, for I think I just have, but a lot of blooming good it will do me as I already have another building project in mind and I'm going to want every one of the talented buggers to come back.

CHAPTER TWENTY TWO

WAITING FOR KATE

Even though spring came to my meadow I continued to write because I thoroughly enjoyed it. All of the funny and wonderful things which had happened since we first came to Ireland were too precious to lose through faulty memory and I wanted to put them to paper while they were still fresh in my mind.

I was writing away one day when Peter Kelly, my quantity surveyor, stopped by and suggested I join the Tralee Scribblers group. He even offered to take me to the next scheduled meeting. I went, and was delighted to meet people who were real writers. That first evening everyone read selected pieces of their work. I listened in awe and considered that maybe I needed some remedial courses before I would feel comfortable in this group. But they invited me to join and I couldn't resist and two weeks later I summoned up the courage to read from a chapter of my book.

I was very anxious about reading and sharing my writing, because if they didn't like it I would have spoiled for myself the pleasure of writing for ever. But if I didn't read I would never be able to go forward and improve so I had a challenge – and me and challenges – of course I took it.

So I read my piece and the response from the seasoned veterans was fantastic. They laughed in all the right places and gave me excellent suggestions. I had faced my first writing critics and received praise, constructive criticism and encouragement to go on. So I wrote more and more of my own little book which really became less and less of my own private pleasure, as I started to share my Irish experiences with the Tralee Scribblers group. They joined me in the fun and laughter and at each meeting they almost screamed encouragement by saying "Don't stop now, we want to hear the rest." So I kept writing the rest.

Another guest season and winter went by. I wrote whenever I had a chance but I always had the feeling I really wanted to do something more constructive to improve my writing skills. Unless I got encouragement all the time, I found I doubted my ability because I'd never had any formal education in writing.

Well actually I had a little. Years before I had taken one short course in creative writing. I had taken the course, not by choice but accidentally, because I needed three more English credits for my university degree. All the upper level classes were filled and the only course left open in the English Department was "Creative Writing." I had to get special permission from the Dean to take the course and have the credits apply towards my degree requirements.

The course was in the evening and taught by an ex-nun who was delightfully and shockingly uninhibited. She was obviously making up for the time lost behind convent walls. I showed up for the first class and found I was the only member of the group who wasn't either an English major or a "hippie". I found the format somewhat unusual as each student was responsible for presenting one evening of creative work and the venue was not a classroom, but was to be our home or favourite wine bar. Liquid refreshments were definitely a course requirement!

This was in the early seventies and I had led a reasonably conservative life. I had never even considered burning my bra nor indeed knew anyone who had done so. It was quite a shock for me to be thrown in with this group. I couldn't protest because I either went along and took the course for the credits or waited another twelve months to receive my degree.

When it was my turn to present the evening, I made sure my husband would be out of town on business. I sent my sons to the neighbours. Then I loaded the large table in the diningroom with lethal punch and lots of food and sat back to wait for everyone to arrive. They all arrived at one time, including the ex-nun, in a beatup van which was covered in peace signs and slogans which included *Make Love Not War, Pot is Good for You* and *Get Out of*

Vietnam. They parked the damn thing right in my driveway in full view of God and all the neighbours and I had to smile and be gracious because I needed the bloody course credits.

Unfortunately my sons spotted the van in the driveway and the first chance they got, they squealed to their ultraconservative father. He had never really believed I was taking an English course as I had been returning from "class" for some weeks with the distinct smell of alcohol on my breath. Oh well, I passed the course and that marriage was on the rocks anyway!

But that had been just one short course in the past. I simply had no experience with writing which was not formal or, to be more precise, I had never written anything people would read for entertainment, as, Lord knows, most of the stuff that comes out of a hospital administration office gets looked at by glazed eyes then dropped in the trash bin.

Then one day I ran into my friend Mary O'Connor and she asked me if I was going to the Listowel Writers Week. This is an international writers' festival, with workshops conducted by professional writers, which is held every year in May. I had never considered going before because the dates were right at the beginning of my guest season. Mary was all excited about it and had already signed up in a workshop to be conducted by Kate Cruise O'Brien. I listened to her for a few minutes in pure envy, then in a flash I said, "Hey, I'm going too – maybe we can ride together."

Once I made the decision to go everything fell into place. Ina found a friend to help her for the days I would be gone and Mary and I worked out a driving schedule between us. I had one initial disappointement. Kate Cruise O'Brien's workshop was already full. I had to take my second choice.

On the first day of the workshop, when we were driving to Listowel, Mary started telling me how nervous she was about going back into the classroom. She was very honest and she was very nervous. When we parted company in the school building in Listowel, Mary went off to her workshop looking much as if she was going to her own execution. I sat in my workshop and in the first thirty minutes knew I was in the wrong place. The workshop was fine, it's just that it wasn't what I was looking for, or had been expecting.

By break-time I was almost sick with disappointment and went looking for Mary to tell her I was going home. I found her in the cafeteria bubbling away, talking and laughing with other members of her workshop. I really didn't need to ask her how she had enjoyed her morning. When I told her my predicament she said, "Why don't you ask Kate if you can join our group – she's standing right over there – just go on and ask her." Well her attitude had certainly changed, from one who had been so apprehensive, there she was bubbling away, calling the well-known journalist and Literary Editor for Poolbeg Press "Kate" as if she had known her all her life!

I hesitated and then thought, "Oh well, what

the hell, I've nothing to lose" and walked over to where "Kate" was standing. I introduced myself and explained my problem. She immediately said, "Just come over to the next session this afternoon." I was so delighted I could have done a Séamus on her – Séamus my dog that is, who pins me with his paws and licks my face all over whenever he is ecstatically happy about something. I decided maybe I'd better not and that possibly I was spending too much time around my dog to have even thought of it!

And Kate went on to say, "I gave a thirty minute writing assignment this morning, and if you would like, you can use your lunch time to catch up as we will be reading them this afternoon."

I tried to look as serious and studious as I could and then I asked, "What's the topic?" She replied, "My Mother – just write for thirty minutes about your mother." My eyes opened wide in shock and my stomach turned over – oh hell, I had spent most of my life trying to avoid or overcome that topic. Why couldn't she have made it "My Summer Holidays" or "My Favourite Pet" or even "Existentialism in Ireland" . . . but "My Mother" . . . oh holy hell!

Anyway, I wrote for thirty minutes and when I finished I was clammy all over just at the thought of reading the stuff out loud. I was sure I would be in a group who would be writing about homemade apple tarts, beautiful hand-made dresses, being tucked in with stories at bedtime – or grey-haired mothers who scrubbed the kitchen floor and said a family rosary every night. And there I would be with my little piece!

Actually the afternoon session wasn't bad at all, in fact it worked out very well. I was not the first to read and while I was listening to the others, it hit me again how true it was that everyone has a story and when that story is written openly, with care and with emotion from the heart – the words come alive. I became so engrossed listening to the power and beauty of everyone else's words, I didn't have a chance to be apprehensive about my own.

* * *

Mary and I were both very pleased with ourselves and our first day in Listowel. Kate had been very generous in her criticism of our work and we chattered away going home in the car. The conversation went something like this:

"What do you think of Kate?" Mary asked.

"She is very good and puts a lot of effort into her workshop," I said.

"She's tough," said Mary, "I think she must have been a school teacher."

"Oh, she's tough enough," said I "I think you're right about her being a school teacher but I think she was a drill sergeant before that."

"She certainly keeps the workshop focused and she really has a great sense of humour but boy she gets upset when anyone walks in late. Did you see the look on her face when yer one walked in the door?"

"God, I'm glad it wasn't me," I said.

"You should show her your book," said Mary.

"Mary, you must be joking – did you hear her talking to that one about format and sentence structure – holy cow, Mary, at this point in my life I wouldn't know an adverb or a past participle if it bit me on the nose. And semi-colons could be a bowel disease. Mary, I don't even get my commas right. Full stops and capitals are as much as I can handle but sometimes I get the apostrophes correct."

"I still think you should show it to her. She liked your piece this afternoon."

"Mary, that's because she couldn't see how it was written, she could only hear me read – have you ever read any of her newspaper columns? Mary, that one's serious stuff. I don't think she would be impressed at all with the fact that I don't use commas because I don't know where in the hell to put them."

"I think your book is good. I didn't notice that you didn't have any commas."

"Well I use some here and there but I usually go with the philosophy 'When in doubt – don't' and I have a lot of don'ts."

"I still think you should show her your book."

"Mary, for heaven's sake – would you show her yours?"

"Well, maybe you're right."

The next morning we were up and out early to

make sure we would not be late. When Kate came in the door of the classroom we were already seated at our desks. She looked around and counted heads, assessed the fact that one was missing and from the look on her face I was glad again it wasn't me. She spoke for a while, then gave us another writing assignment. This time the topic was "My Father" and we had to describe one or more incidents which would give a reader a descriptive picture of what our fathers were like. I sat and thought, then thought some more.

All of the things I remember most about my father are funny, there are simply no bad things which jump to mind when I think of him. And that morning, trying to think of which incident would best describe him, I suddenly remembered his pig. He had, totally out of the blue, decided to raise pigs so God only knows where he bought one, but he did and put it out in his backyard. The pig survived exactly part of one night. It was found in the morning belly up with four feet in the air, frozen stiff. My father was really upset about this as he was convinced someone had sold him a bum pig. It just didn't occur to him that being in Kansas City, Missouri with the temperature ten degrees below zero the night before might have had anything to do with it! The poor bloody pig died before my father had got to page two of his pig farming manual. The full story of my dad and the pig is so hilarious it is impossible to even think of all these years later without the tears running down my face from laughter.

So that morning when I was writing my pig story for Kate I was convulsed over the desk. I tried to pull myself together and write without disturbing the others but I was snorting and choking, trying not to laugh out loud and the tears just kept streaming down my face onto my notepaper.

When the thirty minutes were up Kate said "Well, Maureen, you go first as we're all waiting to hear what you've written that's so funny." I dried my eyes and read my piece and drying my eyes had been a waste of time. It didn't matter because when I got through, everyone was laughing just as hard as I was. Kate said she loved the story and complimented me on the style I had used to write it. She went on to say lots of nice things and just when I was doing "a Séamus" listening to her, where if his ears get rubbed or his tummy gets scratched he is transported with pleasure – I heard her say, "You really should work at writing professionally."

I heard Mary O'Connor's voice chime in, "Oh she's already written a book" and Kate said to me "Oh really, what's it about?"

Well I told her I had written about how I came to be an Irish Innkeeper. She listened to me. Then she said the words which stopped my heart: "I'd like to read it." I don't know when my heart started beating again but after a while Mary O'Connor passed me a note "We'll go home at lunch time and get it," it read. I waited a little while and passed back a note which read, "No need to – actually by chance I just happen to have it with me!" Now, will anybody try to tell me there's not magic and little people in North Kerry. I had written a book – or almost a book – and before it was finished, an editor for a publishing company had said she'd like to read it!

At the lunch break I casually walked up to Kate's desk to hand her my book. But she looked at my manuscript and said, "It's going to have to be bound." And just when my heart was on its way to my boots she said, "There's a place down the road where you can get it done – give it to me later." Mary and I ran like rabbits down the road and found the office supply store and got the manuscript bound before we could even think of swallowing a mouthful of lunch.

Even with the manuscript bound I couldn't swallow a mouthful and I sat there watching Mary eat and I said terribly intelligent things like, "Oh God, Mary, do you believe this? What if she changes her mind? What if when we go back she's forgotten all about it? What if she reads it and doesn't like it?"

Mary, in between mouthfuls, kept saying, "She'll love it." And when she finished her plate, she put her knife and fork together and said, "Look, we'll lie down in front of her car until she takes the book." I remember saying, "Mary I think she walked this morning."

And Mary said "That's all right, we'll lie down on the pavement." And I said, "Do you think she'd think we were being too pushy if we did that?"

We paid our bill and went to hear the author Maeve Binchy speak. Darn, she was good, she addressed a full auditorium and had each and every one of us totally entranced. She also spoke about her new bestseller *The Glass Lake* and said that the film crew was looking for a house with the right location to use as a set for the movie. She asked the audience if anyone knew of a place which sounded like the description in the book to please contact her. As we were walking from the hall back to our classroom Mary said, "You know, Barrow House is on the water and it's a big old house. I wonder if maybe you should call her". I confided that the same thought had crossed my mind also but that my first concern was getting the book into Kate's hands.

Kate didn't arrive in the classroom until bang on the dot of the hour and then started right into the work session so I couldn't give her my book. When class was over there were several people who went up to talk to her and ask questions. Mary and I tried not to look conspicuous as we hovered by the door. Finally, when she started to walk towards the hallway I got my chance. "Oh, Kate," I said as I held out the book. "Do you want me to send this to the office or do you just want to take it now?" Oh God! She hesitated and I really knew my heart would show as a straight line on a cardiac monitor. And then she reached out, took the manuscript, put it in her carry-all bag and said, "I'll just take it with me and read it when I get back to Dublin and I'll call you".

Mary and I laughed, screamed and laughed again all the way to Barrow. We went straight to the Tralee

Golf Club, ordered champagne and lobster and laughed with utter joy all over again. I vowed it didn't matter if Kate told me my book was the worst trash she had ever read or that it was the most poorly written illiterate garbage without commas she had ever been subjected to. It didn't matter one bit because we were so bloody happy. At least she was going to read the book and how many writers get to know an editor actually saw their work before it was rejected? We were so euphoric we even waved in some friends we spotted out the window on the golf course. When Marion and Don Boxer saw us frantically jumping up and down waving to them from the window, they dropped their clubs and hurried in, in time for our champagne toast to absent friends. Yes, we all stood up and raised our glasses and I solemnly intoned as best I could, "God Bless my Daddy's Pig". And we fell over the table laughing once again.

* * *

The next day, even though we were feeling a little poorly and fragile around the edges, we were back to class on time. But it was the last day and even though it had only been a three day course it was obvious we all were sad it was to end. We had listened to each other's readings and shared a part of ourselves that probably we had never, ever shared with others. Kate did not even glower frostily when "yer one" walked in the door a great deal later than the day before. And we really didn't want to leave the group, or Kate, who really had become so important to us. She had become our very special person because she was a "real" writer who was successful and yet she spoke as one of us, encouraged us, never harshly criticised, always pointed out our strengths and gave suggestions how to overcome any weaknesses which interfered with the clarity of what we wished to say. She was just one hell of a "lady" and we all knew it. And even if she probably had been a school teacher or a drill sergeant at some time in the past, we also would have bet our bottom dollar the surliest of marines would simply have said "Yes Ma'am" and slunk to the rear!

We reluctantly said our goodbyes at the end of class and, trying to delay the inevitable, repaired to the bar of the Listowel Arms to try to recapture the sense of fun and excitement of the previous days. Kate joined us and we all decided that there really was no reason for this to be the end as we could all get together for a workshop at Barrow House. Kate agreed. And then they all left to catch trains or buses or simply to drive back home to Dublin. Mary and I sat and looked at each other over our untouched drinks and I said, "Okay, let's drink up and go for a walk."

As we walked out into the square, I looked across the street and saw a bookstore. Immediately I remembered Maeve Binchy and the house by the lake so I said, "Mary, let's see if they have Maeve Binchy's book" so she said "ok" and we walked over to look in the window. We looked at the window display and I think we must have both spotted it at the same time because we let out a shriek simultaneously. There in the window was a copy of *The Glass Lake* and on the cover was a sketch of a house sitting right on the water and, bloody hell, if it wasn't Barrow House looking right back at us. Whoever sketched that drawing had to have been sitting right across the bay at Barrow — it was totally incredible but it was there before our very eyes.

Nostalgia, melancholia or whatever for the group was gone in an instant. Hey, we had the film set for Maeve Binchy's book. We stood on the sidewalk outside that bookstore and made enough noise to frighten children and horses in most of the county, let alone sedate walkers on the streets of the town. After a few seconds, we realised that there were other people around and that they were looking at us strangely. But we looked at each other again and burst out roaring with laughter because the last few days had been so incredible, so totally, utterly incredible and now we were looking at Barrow House on the cover of Maeve Binchy's bestselling book.

The bookstore was closed and it was Saturday night. There wasn't a chance in hell we could wait until Monday morning to buy a copy. To the side of the shop window was a doorway with a bell. Mary laid her finger on it and didn't let it up until someone appeared. He was the tenant of the flat over the shop and, while he couldn't help us to get a book, he told us where the owner of the bookstore lived. We followed his directions and went to his house.

We rousted out the owner and he didn't complain a bit about going down town to open his shop to sell us two books. He also didn't say a word when we passed a newsagent's shop on the way back which was open and had a very large display of the very same book in the window. We must have been so excited we just hadn't noticed it. We made our purchase, then went back to the bar at the Listowel Arms and showed the book cover to some of our acquaintances. There was still a big crowd around from the Writers' festival who had all heard Maeve Binchy speak. Before long Mary and I were surrounded by people who wanted to look at the cover and compare it with the brochure for Barrow House. Everyone was buying us drinks and it didn't take long for the set location for the movie to be definitely decided as Barrow House. And people were looking for parts as extras in the crowd scenes!

On the way home Mary and I talked and laughed so hard we suddenly realised we were on a stretch of road we didn't recognise and sure enough we were lost. We eventually found Tralee and from there we did fine. When I got home Ina was waiting and wanted to know if Kate had said anything about my book. I told her there wasn't a chance there would have been time to have read it yet and went on to tell her all about the location for the movie. She listened to me in silence and then picked up the book – looked through it briefly and wanted to know what part she was going to get because she certainly wasn't going to be just an extra.

When I got into bed that night I was exhausted and ached all over from having laughed for almost two days. I turned out the light and snuggled down between the sheets with my face in the pillow and started to savour the events of the last few days in my mind. Then it suddenly hit me that, maybe just to be sure, I should take a look in the book to find a description of the house. I found it in the first chapter and I knew all was not well when I found a paragraph which stated, "Sister Madeleine was a hermit". Well, Sister Madeleine, God bless her, lived in the house by the lake which was falling down and had all kinds of injured wild animals she took care of. I closed the book and turned off the light again. Yes, it's true. You just can't tell a book by its cover and none of us were going to be in the movies!

* * *

The next morning at breakfast I met all the guests who were staying in the house. Ina had told everyone where I had been and about Kate and my book. They were all so genuinely excited about it I pulled out the champagne and we made the meal brunch instead of breakfast. One couple were supposed to be leaving that morning but they told me there wasn't a chance they could miss all the excitement. If I didn't have room for them they would sleep in their car in the courtyard.

The next day all the guests went off to play golf or sight-see and as each group arrived home they came running over to the diningroom to ask if I had heard anything from Kate. When I told them "No" they were disappointed and all of them said something along the line of "How can you stand it?"

And I just laughed and said, "Well, I have to be realistic and give her time to read it", to which they all responded something along the line of "God, if it was me I'd be a basket case." There was genuine awe and admiration for my cool and calm composure. I went to bed early that night and was reading more about Sister Madeleine with the falling down house when Allan came into the bedroom and said "Guess who's on Questions and Answers tonight? Kate Cruise O'Brien."

I jumped out of bed and yelled, "What the hell's she doing on television when she's supposed to be home reading my book?" Oh well so much for the cool, calm and collected!

The next days grew progressively longer. The guests from the weekend finally had to leave but they insisted on leaving me addresses to let them know how it turned out and some even said they would call long distance. By Thursday whenever the phone rang and it was for reservations I wanted to scream, "Get off the damn phone, I'm expecting a call."

Ina kept asking me, "Are you sure she said she'd

call you?" And I kept hoping that the saying "No news is good news" was actually true.

The days got longer and longer and, by the weekend, I knew that the book was so awful, Kate didn't want to embarrass me by telling me so. Either that or she had forgotten all about it or put it in a pile of manuscripts to read later. And mine was down at the bottom and I'd be very old and senile before she ever got to it.

The following Tuesday evening Ina and I went out to dinner and it was late when I got home. So late in fact that I lay down on the bed with my clothes on and went sound asleep. Morning came too soon and when I heard Allan stirring I just wanted to put my head under the covers for another few hours.

He must have spotted some sign of life from my side of the bed because he said, "You had two phone calls last night while you were gone." I mumbled "Was it anything important?" And he replied somewhat offhandedly, "Well one was for reservations and the other was from Kate." I was out of the bed in an instant screaming, "Kate! My God, what did she say?"

Allan came dangerously close to being strangled when he replied, "Oh I wrote it down – it's all on your desk along with the note about the reservations." I yelled, "What did she say? What did she say? Did she like it? Don't make me wait to find my glasses – *tell me now!*"

I should have known Allan had planned all night

how he was going to tell me because his face broke into a lovely grin and he said, "She loved it and I wrote down everything she said and you're supposed to call her this morning".

I ran into walls and doors scrambling for my glasses which was really surprising as I only wear glasses for reading and don't normally have trouble finding my way around the house. I read Allan's note as best I could and then made him sit down while I interrogated him about every word. "What did she sound like when she said that? Did she sound like she meant it? Or did she sound as though she was just being nice?" Finally Allan refused to answer any more questions and told me to just call Kate that morning as she had requested.

Thank God I had gone to bed the night before in my clothes, otherwise I would have gone charging through the guest dining-room in my pyjamas to find Ina. When I screamed the news to her there was simply too much noise going on in the kitchen. I had to explain to the guests the cause of the excitement. And yes it was champagne time again for everyone and it was only eight in the morning!

It was a group decision not to return Kate's call until the civilised hour of 9 am and we whooped and hollered until 8.45 am. Then we all went silent and watched the clock! At the dot of the hour I picked up the phone, dialled her number and with Ina and a multinational group of listeners waiting with silent intensity – I got the damn answering machine and I hung up. We repeated the performance at 9.30 am and at 10 am with the same results. At 10.15 am we asked Allan to run to town for more champagne. At 11 am I decided that I should put a message on her answering machine so she would know I had returned her call and I prayed she had not taken an early flight to Fiji for a three week holiday.

The phone rang many times in the next few hours and it was all for reservations. Each time it rang we all jumped, then froze while we waited for Ina to answer it and listen to her say in her best modulated tone, "Good morning, Barrow House." We watched for the movement of her head which would indicate, "Relax, it's only reservations". It was two hours of agony but the champagne helped. And then Kate called!

It was an instant trip over the moon. I don't think I heard half of what she said and I'm certain I babbled like an idiot, but it was all right because I was sure she was used to this and she was laughing. She told me she would send me a fax outlining all the suggestions she had and all the things I needed to do, but the bottom line was I had a book which, if I took it seriously and worked hard, was publishable. I readily volunteered to crawl through hot coals of fire or fields of molten lead which Kate said really wasn't necessary and suggested I just read her fax over carefully when I got it and to go from there.

When I received the fax later that afternoon I devoured every word of compliment and of criticism and constructive advice, and then I got to the part of suggested material to be included and top of the list was "Mother". I immediately called back "coals of fire" and "fields of molten lead" and vowed I would not write about my mother. I had written a book or the framework of one. Kate said it had to be twice as long. But what I had written was fun and pleasure and not really about me at all but about Barrow House.

My joy and delight at the prospect of being published faded with the thought of having to include my mother. It was a topic I rarely discussed and had handled by tucking far away. I cursed myself for having written anything about my mother at Listowel and then I cursed my mother for messing with my life once again. And then I sat and looked at my mountains and thought back over all of the things which happened since I first had used them for pleasure and comfort and joy. And slowly I knew the answer and that yes, I would write about my mother for she was definitely part of my story and it was time to stop running away.

So I sat down and wrote the first part of my story again and when I was through there was a peace in my joyous meadow which had never been there before. What can I say but God bless my daddy's pig and yes, God bless my mother too!

CHAPTER TWENTY THREE

THE RIVER

So I have told you my story of how I became an Irish innkeeper. I have read these pages many times, and have enjoyed reliving my memories, but I've remembered so many other people and events which have not been included, I am probably going to have to write a sequel. But there is one story I was saving till last. It is something that has no explanation and in having no explanation is a story in itself.

In my early twenties, when I was living in Missouri, I dreamt one night that I was beside a beautiful river – no, not the Missouri river. This river was not overly wide and had golden sand on each bank. Although I could not see it, I knew that the ocean was over the hills on the far side from where I was standing. In my dream I felt wonderfully warm and happy. My skin was tingling with heat in the most pleasurable way, so much so that, when I woke, I felt great sadness as the sense of that heat slipped away from my body. I had the same dream maybe six or seven times in a twenty-year period. Although nothing happened in my dream – I just stood beside the river and looked at the colours of the scenery, and the flow of the water – it was the most beautiful and sensual dream I could possibly imagine. Even though I only had it on rare occasions, I would feel the greatest pleasure and delight when I realised that I was slipping into my river dream.

After the first dream I thought I could remember everything perfectly, but it was only when I slipped into it again that I could really see the colours and feel the wondrous sensation. There was no comparison between recall and actually being there. One aspect of the dream slightly confused me. After the first few times the river changed direction. Now this dream, even from the first time I had it, was so vivid that I was convinced the river existed somewhere. And because the river at the beginning flowed north to south, I was sure it had to be in California, because I knew the ocean was over beyond the hills. Although I had never been to California when I first started having this dream, I was convinced I had to have seen it somewhere in a movie or travelogue. That was until it changed its direction of flow.

Then one day in June, in my second year as an Irish innkeeper, I made what was a most astonishing discovery. Sally Kabrick, a very dear friend from my Missouri days, was visiting for a few weeks. It was a gloriously warm sunny day, and we decided to put on our bathing suits and take the little puppies, Paddy and Séamus, for a walk on the beach. The tide in the bay was going out, so we walked towards the mouth of the channel at Fenit Island. It was one of those summer days in Ireland, where the sun was shining and the colours all around were the most brilliant vibrant shades an eye could hope to see. I felt the glorious sunshine on my body, and I turned to look at the scenery behind me, and there I was suddenly in the middle of my dream.

My river had never been a river at all. It had been the tide in the deep channel flowing in and out of the bay, and the hills with the ocean beyond. Yes, over the hills was Tralee Bay, part of the Atlantic Ocean, where my little village of Kilfenora is situated. There in front of me was my beautiful river and my skin was warm and deliciously tingling from the sun. It was my dream but I wasn't going to have to lose it by waking up. I was living it.

It is difficult to describe my emotions and thoughts. I didn't have the sense of shock and surprise I had had when I first saw my mountains again. Then I had been totally stunned because I had completely obliterated them from my conscious memory. But this was different. I'd only ever in my life stood in this spot in a dream. All recognition came only from that. I have trawled my memory many times since and the answer is always the same. There isn't a chance I could have ever been in that spot before that day in June!

No, I wasn't shocked or stunned, I was simply speechless and surprised. I felt the most incredible sense of tranquillity and joy – not bursting, jumping up and down joy. And maybe joy is the wrong word. How do I describe an intense feeling of being at one with the world, and the wonderful sense of eternity and belief in God with His mysterious and wondrous ways?

At that point I had owned Barrow House for seven years, and had watched the tide come in and out many, many times. But it wasn't until that day, standing in that spot, with the sun tingling on my skin, that I realised what I was looking at. And now, do you understand why I can so easily say that I really never had a choice about coming to Barrow House? I can't explain it, nor am I even going to try, and if anyone can come up with an answer please write to me. But please, please, don't anyone suggest that in my previous life I was a salmon. I have already thought of that and don't much like the idea at all, at all.

Yes, I can laugh at what has happened to my life. I left Ireland long ago to go out into the world, hoping to do it all. And, to be honest, there is not much that I've missed, except by my choice. And now I'm free of all of those things, and I can laugh about it all in the most comfortable way. Here I am back in Ireland just as my grandmother said, and the most beautiful dream of my life was right under my nose for years before I saw it.

And now when I see the first bluebell of the year, smell the mayflower or see the sunrise on a beautiful

Irish morning, I can shriek with delight and suffer no embarrassment. When the moon is full and dancing over my mountains I can turn loose my ancient druid blood, and howl without shame for my pagan instincts, because even though He had a Jewish son, I know God is an Irishman who never emigrated and was always waiting here. And when as a child you have lived by the sea with the mountains to greet you in the morning, with water from the stream in the meadow, heat from a turf fire, light from the moon or paraffin lamp, and a grandmother who was a witch, you just know all of these things.

But grandmother dear, it's not that I'm complaining, but years ago when you told me you saw me living in a big white house in Ireland, with people all around me, could you not have made it President Mary Robinson's place in the Park? If not that, could you not have thrown in a large inheritance, a few maids, a gardener and, most of all, some one to cook breakfast!

Yes, Grandmother, I came back but –

HELP, I'm an Irish innkeeper!!